Speaking Out: Issues and Con...
各抒己见

Speaking Out: Issues and Controversies 各抒己见 is an advanced Chinese language textbook that explores topics such as human nature, moral values, mass consumption, Western influences, and technological innovation. In presenting subjects that reflect major concerns in contemporary China, the book invites students to reflect upon the forces shaping modern Chinese society.

This textbook presents ten lessons in five units entitled "Constancy and Change," "Joy and Sorrow," "Right and Wrong," "Chinese Tradition and Western Influence," and "New and Old." These pairs of opposites conjure up an ever-changing world of ebb and flow, a world that stimulates learners' imaginations and arouses their enthusiasm for open dialogue and lively discussion.

Concise in language and with lessons in both simplified and traditional characters, the textbook is a valuable aid for university students interested in passing the HSK Level VI or attaining ACTFL advanced-level proficiency. Accompanying audio recordings can be found online at www.routledge.com/9780367902704.

Hsiao-wei Rupprecht is Associate Professor, Teaching Stream and Coordinator of the Chinese Language Program in the Department of East Asian Studies at the University of Toronto. She holds a Ph.D. in East Asian Languages and Literature from the University of Wisconsin at Madison. She has taught Chinese language and literature in North America, Germany, China, and Taiwan for thirty years. Her publications include *Language through Literature: An Advanced Reader of Contemporary Chinese Short-Short Stories* (2010) and *Departure and Return: Chang Hen-shui and the Chinese Narrative Tradition* (1988).

Jianhua Shen holds an M.A. in Chinese and has taught Chinese in the United States since 2001. She is currently Senior Lector in Chinese at Yale University.

Gang Pan is Assistant Professor, Teaching Stream at York University in Toronto. He holds a Ph.D. in East Asian Studies, with a collaborative specialization in Sexual Diversity Studies, from the University of Toronto. His research interests include modern and contemporary Chinese literature and culture, narratology and semiotics. He teaches Chinese language, modern and pre-modern Chinese literature, modern Chinese drama, Chinese cinema and Chinese martial arts culture.

Yanfei Li is Lecturer at the University of Toronto. She holds a Ph.D. in East Asian Studies from the University of Toronto and a B.A. in Comparative Literature and Cultural Studies from Tsinghua University. Her research focuses on modern and contemporary Chinese literature, cultural studies of heritage and urban history. She teaches all levels of Chinese language, all genres of Chinese literature, contemporary Chinese film culture and urban cultural studies.

Yu Wen is a Ph.D. candidate in the Department of East Asian Studies at the University of Toronto. Her research interests include Chinese literature and culture, traditional Chinese poetics and aesthetics, and medieval Chinese poetry and prose. She currently teaches second-year Chinese.

Speaking Out: Issues and Controversies
各抒己见
An Advanced Chinese Reader 汉语高级读本

Hsiao-wei Rupprecht, Jianhua Shen, Gang Pan, Yanfei Li, and Yu Wen

LONDON AND NEW YORK

First published 2021
by Routledge
2 Park Square, Milton Park, Abingdon, Oxon OX14 4RN

and by Routledge
52 Vanderbilt Avenue, New York, NY 10017

Routledge is an imprint of the Taylor & Francis Group, an informa business

British Library Cataloguing-in-Publication Data
A catalogue record for this book is available from the British Library

Library of Congress Cataloging-in-Publication Data
Names: Rupprecht, Hsiao-wei Wang, author.
Title: 880-01 Speaking out : Issues and Controversies : an Advanced Chinese
   Reader = Ge shu ji jian : Han yu gao ji du ben / Hsiao-wei Rupprecht,
   Jianhua Shen, Gang Pan, Yanfei Li, Yu Wen. Other titles: 880-02 Ge shu ji jian:
   Han yu gao ji du ben
Description: New York : Routledge, 2020. | Includes indexes. | Chinese and English.
Identifiers: LCCN 2020008352 (print) | LCCN 2020008353 (ebook)
Subjects: LCSH: Chinese language—Readers.
Classification: LCC PL1117 .R87 2020 (print) | LCC PL1117 (ebook) |
   DDC 495.186—dc23
LC record available at https://lccn.loc.gov/2020008352
LC ebook record available at https://lccn.loc.gov/2020008353

ISBN: 978-0-367-90269-8 (hbk)
ISBN: 978-0-367-90270-4 (pbk)
ISBN: 978-1-003-02348-7 (ebk)

Typeset in Times New Roman
by Apex CoVantage, LLC

Visit the eResources: www.routledge.com/9780367902704

Contents 目录

第五单元
新与旧   101

Figures 插图目录

Lesson summaries

第1课 《三字经》选读

This lesson's writing, an excerpt from the classic Chinese text the *Three-Character Classic*, presents the view that human nature is intrinsically good and changes only under the influence of the environment.

第2课 质疑"制度崇拜"

This lesson's essay argues that laws and regulations alone cannot create a civil, safe and respectful Chinese society.

第3课 大过年的烦心事

This lesson's essay highlights a dilemma faced by Chinese couples made up of only children: whether to celebrate the Chinese New Year at the home of the husband's or the wife's parents.

第4课 大学生竞聘搓澡工、淘粪工、环卫工是喜还是忧？

This lesson's essay presents opposing perspectives on the phenomenon of university graduates taking up manual work in China's competitive job market.

第5课 爱心恐惧症

This lesson's essay presents arguments both for and against offering assistance to elderly people who appear injured or ill in public.

第6课 地动山摇中的选择

This lesson's essay centers around the true story of a teacher who abandoned his students and fled for his own safety during an earthquake. It presents opposing views of the morality of his actions.

第7课 洋节在中国

This lesson's essay presents the pros and cons of celebrating Western holidays in China.

第8课 星巴克引发的争议

This lesson's essay presents arguments in favor and against allowing a Starbucks coffee shop in or near an ancient Chinese cultural site.

第9课 光棍节与网购

This lesson's essay describes mass online consumption during China's "Singles' Festival" and sheds light on the root cause of this seemingly exuberant phenomenon, namely, the imbalance in China's male-to-female birth ratio.

第10课 微信与中国新经济

This lesson's essay argues that WeChat, China's multipurpose messaging and mobile payment app, reflects a chief characteristic of China's new economy, namely, the wedding of technological growth and consideration for human wellbeing.

Preface

In North America, there is a dearth of instructional material for advanced Chinese language students. To create their course packs, instructors often assemble material from a hodgepodge of sources, including the few advanced Chinese language textbooks currently available. Although these textbooks typically provide useful background material on Chinese culture and society, they do not directly address pressing contemporary concerns. Furthermore, most advanced textbooks emphasize reading, listening and writing over speaking. It was against this background that we compiled *Speaking Out: Issues and Controversies*.

Nine of the ten lesson essays in this textbook center around a contemporary social or cultural topic. We recognize that China is changing so rapidly that any textbook that deals with contemporary issues is bound to become dated in some respects eventually. With that in mind, we tried our best to include essays that highlight either timeless ethical or moral questions (for example, the nature of human goodness, the conflict between altruism and selfishness) or social and cultural phenomena which are likely to persist and remain relevant for some time to come (for example, mass consumption and the tension between traditional and Western values).

This textbook's emphasis on speaking also distinguishes it from other advanced textbooks currently in use. Debate exercises are an essential feature of this book. These exercises teach students how to present convincing arguments and engage debate opponents in Chinese. They provide questions or hints for both sides to consider in formulating their arguments. Three lessons give examples of how to defend a position; five lessons present examples of how to argue both sides of an issue. In our fourth-year Chinese course at the University of Toronto, the debates have been the activities that our students have most welcomed and enjoyed.

This textbook could serve equally well as either a primary or a supplementary textbook at the university level. In North America, a fourth-year Chinese language course typically has three or four hours of instruction per week, three hours in a fifteen-week semester or four hours in a twelve-week semester. The ten lessons of this textbook, each of which takes roughly four hours to complete, could therefore serve as the primary instructional material in either. Alternatively, each lesson could supplement other instructional material.

It is our hope that this textbook will not only contribute to students' understandings of the "whys" and "hows" of China's economic transformation, but also serve as a stimulus to open dialogue and lively discussion.

Hsiao-wei Rupprecht
University of Toronto
February 10, 2020

Acknowledgments

I must begin by thanking my son, Christoph Rupprecht, who spent countless hours revising and polishing the English translations in numerous drafts of our manuscript. His command of the English language and its subtleties is remarkable; this textbook could not have been completed without his assistance.

My gratitude goes to my collaborators, Jianhua Shen, Gang Pan, Yanfei Li, and Yu Wen, for their wholehearted dedication to this project. The road to publication of this textbook was long and difficult; only with their support was I able to stay the course to the end.

I am also deeply grateful to my old friend, Ming-ming Cheung, who selflessly lent her time, energy and considerable talent to produce the forty illustrations in this textbook. Her memorable caricatures add comic relief to the book's more serious topics.

I am indebted to my fourth-year students at the University of Toronto. In the past six years, they brought to my attention innumerable errors in our manuscript and offered many useful comments and suggestions. Their feedback was invaluable in revising the manuscript and bringing it to completion.

I appreciate very much Shuping Zhang for reading our manuscript and giving us helpful advice. I also thank Mengying Fan and Yu Wen for designing a lively and elegant cover, which captures the spirit of our book. To the University of Toronto's Department of East Asian Studies, I would like to express my thanks for its encouragement and support. Finally, I would like to convey my gratitude to the editorial team at Routledge for their thoroughness and professionalism in guiding our manuscript to publication.

Hsiao-wei Rupprecht
February 20, 2020

第一单元

恒与变

第1课 《三字经》选读

Figure 1.1 孟母三迁
by Mingming Cheung (2020)
© Mingming Cheung.

Figure 1.2 孟母断杼
by Mingming Cheung (2020)
© Mingming Cheung.

Figure 1.3 窦燕山有五子
by Mingming Cheung (2020)
© Mingming Cheung.

Figure 1.4 玉不琢不成器
by Mingming Cheung (2020)
© Mingming Cheung.

人之初, 性本善。性相近, 习相远。
苟不教, 性乃迁。教之道, 贵以专。
昔孟母, 择邻处。子不学, 断机杼。
窦燕山, 有义方。教五子, 名俱扬。
养不教, 父之过。教不严, 师之惰。
子不学, 非所宜。幼不学, 老何为?
玉不琢, 不成器。人不学, 不知义。

第1课《三字經》選讀

人之初, 性本善。性相近, 習相遠。
苟不教, 性乃遷。教之道, 貴以專。
昔孟母, 擇鄰處。子不學, 斷機杼。
竇燕山, 有義方。教五子, 名俱揚。
養不教, 父之過。教不嚴, 師之惰。
子不學, 非所宜。幼不學, 老何為?
玉不琢, 不成器。人不學, 不知義。

【白话译文】

(每个人) 人生的初期, 本性原来是善良的; (大家的) 本性相近, (但是后来受到社会影响,) 习性越来越不同。

如果 (从小) 不教育, (孩子善良的) 本性就会改变。教育的主旨, 最重要的是 (要教孩子) 专心。

以前孟子的母亲, (为了教育孩子,) 选择邻居 (来) 交往。儿子不学习, (孟母) 把 (织布机上的) 梭子折断, (以此告诫 [gàojiè to caution]) 孟子学习不可半途而废 (bàn tú ér fèi to give up halfway)。

燕山 (这个地方有一个) 姓窦 (名禹钧) 的人, (教育孩子) 有 (符合) 道理的方法。(他) 教育五个儿子, (后来他们的) 名声都远扬。

生养 (却) 不教育, (这是) 父亲的过错。教育 (学生) 不严格, (这是) 老师的懒惰。

小孩子不好好学习, 不是合宜的。(如果) 年纪小的时候不学习, 老了还能有什么作为呢?

玉石不琢磨, (就) 不能成器。人不学习, (就) 不会懂得道理。

词语注释

1　《三字经》(Sānzì Jīng Three-Character Classic) 是传统儿童的启蒙读物 (qǐméng dúwù reading material for instructing young children), 每三字一句, 每四句一组, 背诵起来很容易, 像唱儿歌。大多数学者认为作者是南宋 (1127–1279) 王应麟 (Wáng Yìnglín 1223–1296)。

2　人之初, 性本善。性相近, 习相远。

　之　zhī: 在这里相当于现代汉语的 "的" (父母之命 / 回家之路 / 一家之长)
　初　chū: 开始, 这里指人生下来的时候 (初步 / 初级 / 初中 / 五月初五 / 当初)

性 xìng:

    (1) nature; character (本性/性格)
    (2) gender (性别/男性/女性)
    (3) sex (性爱/性病)

本 běn: 本来 (原本/根本)
善 shàn:

    (1) 善良; 好 (善有善报, 恶有恶报/善始善终/善待)
    (2) 善于 (能歌善舞/善变)

相 xiāng: 彼此间的距离 (相近/相远/相隔); 互相 (相约/相爱)
    xiàng: 容貌; 样子 (相貌/长相/照相/相片)

习 (習) xí: 本义是反复做 (练习/复习); 这里指经过重复而形成的习性 (习惯/习俗)

3   苟不教, 性乃迁。教之道, 贵以专。

苟 gǒu:

    (1) 如果 (苟能坚持, 必将胜利)
    (2) 随便 (不苟言笑)

教 jiào: 指导 (教导/请教/教育/教学/教室/教师/教授/教材); 宗教 (教堂/教皇/教士)
    jiāo: 传授 (教书/教中文)
乃 nǎi: 就会 (工作压力太大, 长久乃影响健康)
迁 (遷) qiān: 转变 (变迁/搬迁); 这里指变坏
道 dào:

    (1) 方法 (医道/生存之道/生财有道)
    (2) 路 (道路/街道/道听途说)
    (3) 规律 (道理/道德)

贵 (貴) guì:

    (1) 重要的 (和为贵/贵宾 / 贵客/贵人多忘事)
    (2) 不便宜 (贵重的礼物); "贵" 的反义词是 "贱" (贱卖/贱价)

专 (專) zhuān: 集中在一件事上 (专心/专业/专长/感情专一/专门)

4   昔孟母, 择邻处。子不学, 断机杼。

昔 xī: 过去, 以前 (今不如昔/今昔对比/昔日)
孟母: 孟子的母亲
孟子 (约公元前372–约公元前289年), 名轲, 鲁国邹 (今山东省邹城市)
人, 他是战国时期 (公元前475–公元前221) 伟大的思想家、教育家。
他是儒家学派的代表人物, 与孔子并称 "孔孟"。
邻 (鄰) lín: 接近; 附近 (邻国/邻家/邻近); 这里指邻居
处 (處) chǔ: 交往 (相处); 境地 (处境), 多指不利的情况; 办理 to handle (处理日常事务)
    chù: 地方 (所到之处/处所/到处/处处)
断 (斷) duàn: 折断
机 (機) 杼 jīzhù; 机: 织布机 loom; 杼:梭子suōzi shuttle

5　窦燕山, 有义方。教五子, 名俱扬。

　　窦燕山 (竇燕山) Dòu Yānshān: 燕山这个地方一个姓窦的人
　　义 (義) yì:

　　　　(1) 合宜的, 合乎公益的 (义举/义演)
　　　　(2) 公正合宜的道理 (正义/道义)

　　方 fāng: 方法
　　名 míng: 名声
　　俱 jù: 都
　　扬 (揚) yáng: 传播出去; 传播开 (惩恶扬善/发扬/声名远扬)

6　养不教, 父之过。教不严, 师之惰。

　　养 (養) yǎng:

　　　　(1) 提供生活品或生活费用 (赡养 shànyǎng to support one's parents/抚养 fǔyǎng to raise one's children)
　　　　(2) 教育 (培养/教养)
　　　　(3) 培植花草、饲养动物 (养花/养猪/养狗)

　　过 (過) guò:

　　　　(1) 错误 (过错/过失)
　　　　(2) 从这里到那里 (过马路/过程/经过)
　　　　(3) 超出 (过度/过剩/过高/过多/过分/有过之而无不及/聪明过人)
　　　　(4) 表示曾经或是已经 (看过/用过)

　　严 (嚴) yán: 严格
　　师 (師) shī: 老师
　　惰 duò: 懒 (懒惰/惰性)

7　子不学, 非所宜。幼不学, 老何为?

　　宜 yí:

　　　　(1) 应该 (不宜劳累过度/事情宜早不宜迟)
　　　　(2) 适合 (适宜/景色宜人/世界上最宜居住的地方)

　　幼 yòu: 年纪小的时候
　　老何为 (老何為) lǎo hé wéi: 长大以后还能做什么? 长大以后还有什么用?

8　玉不琢, 不成器。人不学, 不知义。

　　玉 yù

　　　　(1) 玉石/玉器
　　　　(2) 美 (亭亭玉立)

　　琢 zhuó: 雕刻 diāokè to chisel; to carve
　　器 qì

　　　　(1) 用具 (器具/木器/机器)
　　　　(2) 人的才干 (大器晚成)

孟母三迁 (简体)

从前孟子小的时候, 父亲早早地就死了, 母亲守节没有改嫁。一开始, 他们搬到靠近墓地的地方去住。孟子就和邻居的小孩一起学着大人跪拜、哭嚎的样子, 玩起了办丧事的游戏。孟母看到了, 皱起眉头说: "不行! 我不能让我的孩子住在这里了!" 于是她就带着孟子搬到市集上靠近杀猪宰羊的地方去住。到了市集, 孟子又和邻居的小孩一起学起商人做生意和屠宰猪羊的事。孟母知道了, 又皱皱眉头说: "这个地方也不适合我的孩子居住。" 于是他们搬到了学校附近。在这里, 孟子开始变得守秩序、懂礼貌、喜欢读书。孟母很满意地说: "这才是我儿子应该住的地方呀!" 就在此住下了。

孟母三遷 (繁体)

從前孟子小的時候, 父親早早地就死了, 母親守節沒有改嫁。一開始, 他們搬到靠近墓地的地方去住。孟子就和鄰居的小孩一起學著大人跪拜、哭嚎的樣子, 玩起了辦喪事的遊戲。孟母看到了, 皺起眉頭說: "不行! 我不能讓我的孩子住在這裡了!" 於是她就帶著孟子搬到市集上靠近殺豬宰羊的地方去住。到了市集, 孟子又和鄰居的小孩一起學起商人做生意和屠宰豬羊的事。孟母知道了, 又皺皺眉頭說: "這個地方也不適合我的孩子居住。" 於是他們搬到了學校附近。在這裡, 孟子開始變得守秩序、懂禮貌、喜歡讀書。孟母很滿意地說: "這才是我兒子應該住的地方呀!" 就在此住下了。

新词语

守节	守節	shǒujié	to remain unmarried after the death of one's husband 以前女人要~, 不能改嫁
墓地	墓地	mùdì	graveyard 他死后葬在故乡的~
跪拜	跪拜	guìbài	to kowtow 在佛像前~
哭嚎	哭嚎	kūháo	to cry loudly 大声~/孩子~起来
丧事	喪事	sāngshì	funeral arrangements 办~
皱眉头	皺眉頭	zhòu méitóu	to knit one's brow 皱起眉头/皱着眉头
市集	市集	shìjí	market 也说"集市" 圣诞~/~广场
宰	宰	zǎi	to slaughter ~羊/~牛
屠宰	屠宰	túzǎi	to butcher, to slaughter ~猪羊/~场 (屠宰的场地 slaughterhouse)

断机教子 (简体)

孟子上学期间,有一天还不到放学的时间就已经回到家。孟母正在织布机前织布,经询问以后,知道孟子逃学了,就很生气。她当着他的面,折断梭子,毁坏了织机上的全部纱线,使自己多日的辛勤劳动毁于一旦。孟子惊恐不解地问母亲为什么要这样。孟母指着织机上断了的纱线说:"你不好好学习,就像被毁坏了的纱线一样,最终会成为废物。" 沉默了一会,孟母压抑着心中的气愤,语重心长地对孟子说:"布是一丝一线织起来的,把梭子折断就织不成布了;读书和织布一样,要靠持之以恒的努力,间断和逃学不能获得渊博的学问,最终必然一无所成。" 孟母用"断机教子"的行动教育了孟子,孟子认识到自己的错误,从而发奋学习,不懈怠,最后成为圣人。

斷機教子 (繁体)

孟子上學期間,有一天還不到放學的時間就已經回到家。孟母正在織布機前織布,經詢問以後,知道孟子逃學了,就很生氣。她當著他的面,折斷梭子,毀壞了織機上的全部紗線,使自己多日的辛勤勞動毀於一旦。孟子驚恐不解地問母親為什麼要這樣。孟母指著織機上被毀壞了的紗線說:"你不好好學習,就像被毀壞的紗線一樣,最終會成為廢物。" 沉默了一會,孟母壓抑著心中的氣憤,語重心長地對孟子說:"布是一絲一線織起來的,把梭子折斷就織不成布了;讀書和織布一樣,要靠持之以恆的努力,間斷和逃學不能獲得淵博的學問,最終必然一無所成。"孟母用"斷機教子"的行動教育了孟子,孟子認識到了自己的錯誤,從而發奮學習,不懈怠,最後成為聖人。

新词语

询问	詢問	xúnwèn	to inquire 父母~我的学习情况/警察~路人车祸的经过
逃学	逃學	táoxué	to cut class 这个孩子~去网吧玩游戏
纱线	紗線	shāxiàn	yarn 用~织布
最终	最終	zuìzhōng	in the end; final 他~承认他错了/我们~目标是取得胜利
废物	廢物	fèiwù	a worthless or useless person; good-for-nothing 他们是一群~
压抑	壓抑	yāyì	to constrain ~着内心的痛苦/~情感
气愤	氣憤	qìfèn	anger; angry 她因~而哭了/市民对食品涨价很~
间断	間斷	jiànduàn	to be interrupted 练习书法不能~
渊博	淵博	yuānbó	(of knowledge) broad and profound 知识~
发奋	發奮	fāfèn	to exert oneself ~学习/~工作
懈怠	懈怠	xièdài	to slack off 不能~
圣人	聖人	shèngrén	sage; wise man 孔子、孟子被尊为~/我们不是~,所以经常做错事

重点词语和句式

1　毁于一旦 (to ruin in a single moment; to be destroyed in a flash; to be wiped out overnight; 旦: 一天)

　　(1)　她当着他的面, 把梭子折断, 毁坏了织机上的全部纱线, 使自己多日的辛勤劳动毁于一旦。
　　　　(Before his eyes, she broke the shuttle and destroyed all of the yarn on the loom. In a single moment, she ruined her hard work of many days.)

　　(2)　那座古城在地震中毁于一旦。
　　　　(That ancient city was destroyed in a flash by an earthquake.)

　　(3)　他们股票投资错误, 多年的积蓄毁于一旦。
　　　　(They invested their money in the wrong stocks; their life savings were wiped out overnight.)

翻译:

　　(1)　The allegations of sexual harassment destroyed that official's career overnight.

　　　　_____

　　(2)　一场大火之中, 他们的家园毁于一旦。

　　　　_____

2　语重心长 (to say in all earnestness)

　　(1)　孟母……语重心长地对孟子说:"布是一丝一线织起来的, 把梭子折断就织不成布了; 读书和织布一样, ……"
　　　　(Mencius' mother . . . said in all earnestness, "Cloth is woven together thread by thread. If you broke the shuttle, you would not be able to finish the cloth. Studying is similar to weaving . . .")

　　(2)　儿子不用功, 母亲语重心长地劝儿子要上进。
　　　　(The son didn't study hard. His mother tried in all earnestness to persuade him to make something out of his life.)

　　(3)　他话不多, 但是语重心长。
　　　　(He didn't say much, but what he did say, he said in all earnestness.)

翻译:

　　(1)　Our teacher encouraged us in all earnestness never to give up in our pursuit of knowledge.

　　　　_____

　　(2)　我的父母总是语重心长地鼓励我努力前进。

　　　　_____

3　持之以恒 (to persevere)

　　(1)　读书和织布一样, 要靠持之以恒的努力。
　　　　(Studying is similar to weaving; it requires perseverance.)

(2) 任何事要成功, 都得持之以恒。

(If you want to succeed at anything, you have to persevere.)

(3) 他是优秀运动员, 我佩服他持之以恒的精神。

(He is an outstanding athlete. I admire him for his perseverance.)

翻译:

(1) To run a marathon requires perseverance. You must keep going no matter how tired you get.

_____

(2) 掌握一门外语不容易, 学习语言必须持之以恒。

_____

4 一无所成 (to accomplish nothing; without accomplishment)

(1) 间断和逃学不能获得渊博的学问, 最终必然一无所成。

(Interrupting your studies and cutting class would ruin your chances of obtaining profound knowledge. In the end, you would certainly accomplish nothing.)

(2) 这个人从小贪玩, 至今一无所成。

(Ever since he was young, this man has enjoyed having fun. To this day, he has accomplished nothing.)

(3) 人要有毅力, 否则一无所成。

(We must have willpower; otherwise, we would accomplish nothing.)

翻译:

(1) Lazy people often accomplish nothing.

_____

(2) 他读书读了二十年, 至今一无所成。

_____

5 从而 (as a result of; so; thereby; 表示结果或进一步的行动)

(1) 孟母用 "断机教子" 的行动教育了孟子, 孟子认识到自己的错误, 从而发奋学习, 不懈怠, 最后成为圣人。

(Mencius' mother taught Mencius a lesson by breaking her shuttle. Mencius realized his mistake. As a result, he studied diligently and did not slack off. In the end, he became a sage.)

(2) 有些作家下乡体验生活, 从而写出来生动的小说反映农民生活。

(Some writers went down to the countryside to experience life there and so were able to write vivid stories that reflected the lives of the peasants.)

(3) 经过多年研究, 他找出了治疗这种病的方法, 从而给予了成千上万病人希望。
(After years of research, he discovered the cure for this disease, thereby giving hope to thousands of patients.)

翻译:

(1) Exercise strengthens the heart, thereby reducing the risk of a heart attack.

_____

(2) 他经常旅游, 从而养成了到处为家的习惯。

_____

练习

一. 用下面的字组词

(1) 性: _____ _____ _____

(2) 本: _____ _____ _____

(3) 相: _____ _____ _____

(4) 习: _____ _____ _____

(5) 教: _____ _____ _____

(6) 专: _____ _____ _____

(7) 处: _____ _____ _____

(8) 过: _____ _____ _____

二. 用以下每题所给的词语写出一段话

(1) 皱眉头 气愤 逃学
(2) 废物 语重心长 间断
(3) 发奋 懈怠 渊博

三. 写作练习

从讨论题目中选择一个问题, 写一篇文章说明自己的观点。字数: 500－700字。

四. 讨论

(1) 你对《三字经》里提到的哪个观点最赞赏?
(2) 《三字经》里的哪个观念你不太同意?
(3) 你认为学校老师的教育和父母的教育, 哪个比较重要?
(4) 你认为什么样的老师是好老师?

(5) 你认为什么样的父母是好父母？

(6) 你对"断机教子"这个故事怎么看？

(7) 你对"孟母三迁"的做法怎么看？你认为环境对人的影响是否很大？

五. 辩论

题目：你认为人性本善还是人性本恶？

正方：人性本善

反方：人性本恶

辩论内容可以考虑以下方面：

什么是人性？人性是天生就有善恶的吗？人性是环境、社会影响而形成的吗？通过后天的教育，人性可以变好或是变坏吗？

第2课 质疑"制度崇拜"

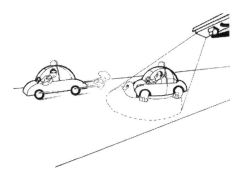

Figure 2.1 司机知道哪里有摄像头，
       就会慢下来
       by Mingming Cheung (2020)

© Mingming Cheung.

Figure 2.2 街上机器监督
       by Mingming Cheung (2020)

© Mingming Cheung.

Figure 2.3 守上帝的法
       by Mingming Cheung (2020)

© Mingming Cheung.

Figure 2.4 中国人优秀的文化
       by Mingming Cheung (2020)

© Mingming Cheung.

今天的社会上有很多问题：有人不喜欢排队，总想插队；公交车上有人就是不给老人让座；有的企业违规排放污染物。对于当下中国很多的问题，有论者动不动就指向制度。对这些人来说，一切社会问题的解决，最后都要仰仗完善制度。好像制度是灵丹妙药，制度一完善，中国就和谐了。这样的想法，可以说是制度崇拜。

很多司机不喜欢遵守交通规则。有人就是不系安全带，有人动不动就超速，还有人乱停车。街上安了摄像头，拍摄违规车辆。这就阻止违规了吗？有的出租车司机慢慢知道了哪里有摄像头，于是在这些地方就很乖；可是一过摄像头，他们立刻恢复原状。你能在街上每隔三米就安一个摄像头吗？

几年前，笔者曾经跟一个德国的环保专家谈到中国的环保问题。他说，中国的环保应该搞得很好啊，因为中国的环保立法已经很完备了。他是以德国的经验，才作出这样的判断。他不知道，这在中国完全是另外一回事。中国的环保问题并不只是法律完不完备的问题，而是即使有了法律，很多企业并不认真遵守。

中国有一句老话，叫做"法令滋彰，盗贼多有"。意思是，法规多了，反倒有更多强盗和小偷。人如果内心失去道德，他就不怕犯法，就会想方设法钻法律的空子。法令再严，也不能弥补道德的缺失。一个社会，如果怀着不轨之心的人太多，法律能有多大作用呢？我们难道不应该反思，制度的完善真有那么灵吗？

法律是显形的道德。人类社会最初并没有法律。法律是人创造的。因为一些人不自觉，所以才有了法律。法律制度不是灵丹妙药，所有的法律都会有漏洞。何况对于聪明的中国人来说，没有什么样的法律是不能被绕开的。上有政策，下有对策，这是中国独有的情况，也是对制度崇拜的讽刺。有时，法律的执行是需要巨大成本的，北京就曾经用机器上街监督随地吐痰的人，后来因为成本太高而不得不放弃。

我们对法律制度的崇拜，源自对西方的肤浅认识。欧美的社会秩序比较好，并非真的是法律本身有那么大的威力。法律是有约束力的，但是以为仅凭法律就能构建有秩序的社会，那是主观臆想。欧美社会有良好的秩序，一个重要的原因就是因为有基督教的伦理作为基础。他们的法制文明，就是建立在这种道德基础上的。为什么他们对工作那么敬业？为什么企业都比较讲诚信？是因为有着对上帝的信仰。美国小孩从小就知道要守上帝的法，到了成年，这种守上帝法的精神就会转化成为遵守社会法律的自觉。虽然今天上帝的观念在欧美很多人心中不再那么强烈，但是基督教文化毕竟影响了几百年，已经深入到了人们的血液里。西方社会不单靠健全的法律制度来维持，还有强大的道德作后盾。

中国不需要上帝, 我们有自己的优秀文化。这种文化让我们注重礼仪, 注重信用, 注重道德。不是不需要完善的法制, 法制的完善一定会推动秩序的建立。中国的法律多如牛毛, 但人们不守法, 就是通过再多的法律也没有太大的益处。当某一部分人不重视法律的时候, 只靠法制是无力的。现在的中国, 冷漠之气胜过了有修养的文化气氛。我们需要法制, 但是如果没有良好的道德作基础、缺少尊重法制的人, 法制只不过是摆设而已。

(节选自小愚观海的博客文章《质疑"制度崇拜"》,
2006年7月3日, 有删改 http://systemupdate.bokee.com/5335433.html)

第2课 質疑"制度崇拜"

今天的社會上有很多問題: 有人不喜歡排隊, 總想插隊; 公交車上有人就是不給老人讓座; 有的企業違規排放污染物。對於當下中國很多的問題, 有論者動不動就指向制度。對這些人來説,一切社會問題的解決, 最後都要仰仗完善制度。好像制度是靈丹妙藥, 制度一完善, 中國就和諧了。這樣的想法, 可以説是制度崇拜。

很多司機不喜歡遵守交通規則。有人就是不繫安全帶, 有人動不動就超速, 還有人亂停車。街上安了攝像頭, 拍攝違規車輛。這就阻止違規了嗎? 有的出租車司機慢慢知道了哪裡有攝像頭, 於是在這些地方就很乖; 可是一過攝像頭, 他們立刻恢復原狀。你能在街上每隔三米就安一個攝像頭嗎?

幾年前, 筆者曾經跟一個德國的環保專家談到中國的環保問題。他説, 中國的環保應該搞得很好啊, 因為中國的環保立法已經很完備了。他是以德國的經驗, 才作出這樣的判斷。他不知道, 這在中國完全是另外一回事。中國的環保問題並不只是法律完不完備的問題, 而是即使有了法律, 很多企業並不認真遵守。

中國有一句老話, 叫做"法令滋彰, 盜賊多有"。意思是, 法規多了, 反倒有更多強盜和小偷。人如果內心失去道德, 他就不怕犯法, 就會想方設法鑽法律的空子。法令再嚴, 也不能彌補道德的缺失。一個社會, 如果懷著不軌之心的人太多, 法律能有多大作用呢? 我們難道不應該反思, 制度的完善真有那麼靈嗎?

法律是顯形的道德。人類社會的最初並沒有法律。法律是人創造的。因為一些人不自覺, 所以才有了法律。法律制度不是靈丹妙藥, 所有的法律都會有漏洞。何況對於聰明的中國人來説, 沒有什麼樣的法律是不能被繞開的。上有政策, 下有對策, 這是中國獨有的情況, 也是對制度崇拜的諷刺。有時, 法律的執行是需要巨大成本的, 北京就曾經用機器上街監督隨地吐痰的人, 後來因為成本太高而不得不放棄。

我們對法律制度的崇拜, 源自對西方的膚淺認識。歐美的社會秩序比較好, 並非真的是法律本身有那麼大的威力。法律是有約束力的, 但是以為僅憑法律就能構建有秩序的社會, 那是主觀臆想。歐美社會有良好的秩序, 一個重要的原因就是因為有基督教的倫理作為基礎。他們的法制文明, 就是建立在這種道德基礎上的。為什麼他們對工作那麼敬業? 為什麼企業都比較講誠信? 是因為有著對上帝的信仰。美國小孩從小就知道要守上帝的法, 到了成年, 這種守上帝法的精神就會轉化成為遵守社會法律的自覺。雖然今天上帝的觀念在歐美很多人心中不再那麼強烈, 但是基督教文化畢竟影響了幾百年, 已經深入到了人們的血液裡。西方社會不單靠健全的法律制度來維持, 還有強大的道德作後盾。

中國不需要上帝, 我們有自己的優秀文化。這種文化讓我們注重禮儀, 注重信用, 注重道德。不是不需要完善的法制, 法制的完善一定會推動秩序的建立。中國的法律多如牛毛, 但人們不守法, 就是通過再多的法律也沒有太大的益處。當某一部分人不重視法律的時候, 只靠法制是無力的。現在的中國, 冷漠之氣勝過了有修養的文化氣氛。我們需要法制, 但是如果沒有良好的道德作基礎、缺少尊重法制的人, 法制只不過是擺設而已。

(節選自小愚觀海的博客文章《質疑 "制度崇拜"》,
2006年7月3日, 有刪改 http://systemupdate.bkee.com/5335433.html)

新词语

质疑	質疑	zhìyí	to query; query ~学校的决定/我对他的学问提出~
制度	制度	zhìdù	system 教育~/投票~
崇拜	崇拜	chóngbài	to worship; worship ~英雄/个人~
插队	插隊	chāduì	to cut in line 别~, 我已经排了半天队了
违规	違規	wéiguī	violation; to break rules and regulations ~通知单/开车~了
排放	排放	páifàng	to discharge; emission 把污水直接~到河里/减少废气 (fèiqì exhaust gas)~
污染物	污染物	wūrǎnwù	pollutant 有害~/空气~
仰仗	仰仗	yǎngzhàng	to rely on; 依靠 ~父母/~工人的支持
灵丹妙药	靈丹妙藥	líng dān miào yào	panacea; miracle cure; 非常灵验、能起死回生的奇药, 比喻幻想中的某种能解决一切问题的有效方法 这不是解决经济问题的~/每天一个苹果, 胜过~
完善	完善	wánshàn	perfect; 完备美好 ~的教学计划/这家旅馆设备很~
和谐	和諧	héxié	harmonious ~的社会/关系~

遵守	遵守	zūnshǒu	to abide by; abidance ~规则/对法律的~
系	繫	jì	to fasten; to tie 腰间~着皮带/把鞋带~上
安全带	安全帶	ānquándài	seat belt 汽车座位~/扣紧~
摄像头	攝像頭	shèxiàngtóu	surveillance camera; 摄: 摄影 高清~/网络~
拍摄	拍攝	pāishè	to shoot a film; to take a picture ~电影/~照片
阻止	阻止	zǔzhǐ	to prevent 他~我说话/~疾病传染/~车祸发生
乖	乖	guāi	well behaved ~孩子/学~了
恢复原状	恢復原狀	huīfù yuánzhuàng	to revert to old ways 他戒酒 (jièjiǔ to abstain from alcohol) 后几天又~了
隔	隔	gé	after an interval of; to be at a distance from ~年/每~一天/相~20米/两家~着一条街
立法	立法	lìfǎ	legislation; legislative 有关公共利益的~/控制~/~会/~程序
完备	完備	wánbèi	complete ~的知识/我们提供~的售后服务
判断	判斷	pànduàn	judgment; to judge 正确的~/~好坏
法令滋彰，盗贼多有	法令滋彰，盗賊多有	fǎlìng zī zhāng, dàozéi duō yǒu	The more laws and regulations, the more robbers and thieves; 出于春秋时期 (770–476 BC) 哲学家老子的《道德经》; 滋: to multiply; to grow ~生/~长; 彰: clear; evident 真理昭~/罪恶昭~; 盗贼: robbers and thieves 抓住~/他家被~光顾过
想方设法	想方設法	xiǎng fāng shè fǎ	to do everything possible; to try all means ~挣钱/~帮助他
钻空子	鑽空子	zuān kòngzi	to take advantage of a loophole; to exploit an advantage; 乘机会 (多指做坏事) 魁北克省的移民项目有漏洞, 有钱的外国人~移民进入加拿大; 钻 zuān to get into; 进入; 空子 kòngzi opening; 指还未占用的地方或时间 找了个空子往里挤/抽个空子到我们这里看一看
弥补	彌補	míbǔ	to make up for ~损失/~过失
缺失	缺失	quēshī	fault; shortcoming 信用的~/这间公司在经营上有许多~
不轨	不軌	bùguǐ	not in accordance with the law; 不守法; literally, straying from the proper path; 轨: 轨道 (track; 这里指 "法律"、"制度") 行为~/~之徒 (徒 tú person; 人)
反思	反思	fǎnsī	to reflect upon; reflection; 思考过去的事情, 从中总结经验教训 ~我们的生活方式/作深刻的~
显形	顯形	xiǎnxíng	explicit in form; 明显露出(的样子) 政治上, 有~的权力 与隐形 (yǐnxíng implicit) 的权力
自觉	自覺	zìjué	conscious; consciousness ~努力不够/出于~
漏洞	漏洞	lòudòng	flaw; literally, leaking hole 这是个~百出的谎言/船上出现~
绕开	繞開	ràokāi	to circumvent; to bypass ~这个话题/~前面的车
对策	對策	duìcè	countermeasure; 对付的策略 想出~/找到~
讽刺	諷刺	fěngcì	satire; to mock 你的不在乎就是对他最大的~/别~他个子矮
执行	執行	zhíxíng	implementation; to implement 计划的~/~命令

成本	成本	chéngběn	prime cost 降低~/提高~
监督	監督	jiāndū	to watch over; supervision 他父母总是~他学习/在老板的~下，员工都不迟到早退了
随地吐痰	隨地吐痰	suídì tǔtán	to spit anywhere in public 请勿~/~没有礼貌
源自	源自	yuánzì	to originate from; 来自 ~内心/~中国传统
肤浅	膚淺	fūqiǎn	superficial 内容~/看法很~
威力	威力	wēilì	power; mighty force 舆论的~/大自然的~
约束	約束	yuēshù	to restrain; restraint ~自己/没有~
构建	構建	gòujiàn	to build; to construct ~和谐的大家庭/~新体系
主观	主觀	zhǔguān	subjective 他很~，从不接受别人的意见
臆想	臆想	yìxiǎng	conjecture; 推测; 主观臆想 (for emphasis): subjective conjecture 你的理论纯粹是主观~/他不知道实情，说的纯属主观~
基督教	基督教	jīdūjiào	Christianity ~的教义来自《圣经》/~徒
伦理	倫理	lúnlǐ	ethics; 原指中国古代音乐的条理，后来比喻封建社会父子、君臣、夫妇、长幼、朋友各类等级的关系以及相应的道德标准。"伦理"与"道德"有时通用，例如"伦理关系"就是"道德关系"~道德/~教育
敬业	敬業	jìngyè	to be dedicated to one's work ~精神/~的专业人士
讲诚信	講誠信	jiǎng chéngxìn	讲: to pay attention; 讲求, 注意; 诚信: integrity; honesty ~是一种美德
信仰	信仰	xìnyǎng	faith; to believe in 坚持自己的~/缺乏~/~基督教/~佛教
毕竟	畢竟	bìjìng	after all 他的发音不准，~他刚开始学习中文
血液	血液	xuèyè	blood 一位来自农村的作家说，他身体里流着农民的~
单	單	dān	only; alone 这件事~靠一个人不行/他能得第一不~凭实力，还靠一点运气
健全	健全	jiànquán	sound; healthy ~的社会/身心~
后盾	後盾	hòudùn	backup support 有父母做~/经济~
礼仪	禮儀	lǐyí	protocol 西方的~/外交~
多如牛毛	多如牛毛	duō rú niú máo	as numerous as the hairs on an ox; innumerable 网上各种信息~/现在的大学生~
冷漠	冷漠	lěngmò	indifferent; 冷淡 性格~/~的态度
修养	修養	xiūyǎng	refinement 有~的人 (有完善的人格, 言行合乎规矩)/有文化~的人 (有文化、艺术知识, 思想达到一定的水平)
气氛	氣氛	qìfēn	atmosphere ~很紧张/欢乐的~
摆设	擺設	bǎishè	objects on display; ornaments 桌子上的小~/这些书只是~

重点词语和句式

1　动不动就 (frequently; at the slightest provocation; 表示很容易做出某种举动)

(1) 对当下中国很多的问题，有论者动不动就指向制度。
(Critics frequently pointed to the system as the cause of many problems in today's China.)

(2) 有些华侨说中文动不动就带上英文字, 听起来真不舒服。
(Some overseas Chinese frequently inject English words into their spoken Chinese. It really sounds annoying.)

(3) 那个父亲动不动就打孩子, 他应该尊重孩子。
(That father beats his child at the slightest provocation. He should respect his child.)

用"动不动就"完成对话:

(1) A: 那两个兄弟相处得怎么样?

B: _____

(2) A: 你的好朋友喜欢上学吗?

B: _____

2　……反倒…… (on the contrary; instead; but; 反而)

(1) 法规多了, 反倒有更多强盗和小偷。
(More laws would not help; on the contrary, they would create more robbers and thieves.)

(2) 她有意做饭露一手, 慌乱中反倒出了错, 把盐放成了糖。
(She intended to show off her cooking skills. Instead, she panicked and made a mistake, substituting sugar for salt.)

(3) 我们尊敬他年岁大, 他反倒跟我们争起来了。
(We respected him because of his age, but he started arguing with us.)

用"……反倒……"完成句子:

(1) 他做任何事都不顺利, 他不找自身原因, 反倒

_____

(2) 知道自己得了癌症以后, 他不悲伤, 反倒

_____

3　……何况……(呢)(what is more; also; let alone)

(1) 法律制度不是灵丹妙药, 所有的法律都会有漏洞。何况对于聪明的中国人来说, 没有什么样的法律是不能被绕开的。
(The law is not a panacea. All laws have their flaws. What is more, there is not a single law that clever Chinese cannot circumvent.)

(2) 我不想去看电影, 我很累, 何况我还在感冒。
(I don't feel like going to the movies. I am tired. Also, I still have a cold.)

(3) 这么复杂的问题, 大人都不懂, 何况孩子呢?
(This is such a complicated issue. It is hard for adults, let alone children, to understand.)

翻译:

(1) 人生就是对对错错, 何况有许多事, 回头看来, 对错已经无所谓了。

_____

(2) 人都会犯错, 何况他还年轻呢?

_____

4 仅凭……就…… (something alone . . .; 只靠……就……)

(1) 如果以为仅凭法律就能构建有秩序的社会, 那是主观臆想。
(If you believed that laws alone could create an orderly society, you would be indulging your imagination.)

(2) 远处传来她的歌声, 仅凭声音, 我们就知道是她。
(The sound of her singing came from afar. From her voice alone, we knew that it was her.)

(3) 她在这行工作了二十年了, 仅凭她的经验就能当经理。
(She has worked in this field for twenty years. Her experience alone qualifies her for the position of manager.)

用"仅凭……就……"完成对话:

(1) A: 他很有天分, 一定能成功。

B: _____

(2) A: 那个企业家白手起家吗?

B: _____

5 建立在……基础上的 (to be built on a foundation of . . .; to be the foundation of . . .)

(1) 他们的法制文明, 就是建立在这种道德基础上的。
(Their justice system is built on such a moral foundation.)

(2) 尊重是一种美德, 和谐的社会是建立在尊重的基础上的。
(Respect is a virtue. A harmonious society is built on a foundation of respect.)

(3) 我们要不断努力, 成功是建立在坚持的基础上的。
(We always have to work hard. Perseverance is the foundation of success.)

翻译:

(1) We have always had faith in each other. Our friendship is built on a foundation of trust.

_____

(2) They have been married for thirty years. Their marriage is built on a foundation of love and mutual respect.

_____

6　就是……再……也……(no matter how . . .)

(1) 中国法律多如牛毛, 但人们不守法, 就是通过再多的法律也没有太大的益处。
(China has a plethora of laws. People do not obey the law. They would not change their behavior, no matter how many laws were passed.)

(2) 他谁的话都不听, 你就是再劝也没用。
(He doesn't listen to anyone. No matter how hard you tried, you would not be able to convince him.)

(3) 我就是工作再忙也找时间运动。
(No matter how busy I am with my work, I find time to exercise.)

用 "就是再……也……" 完成对话:

(1) A: 你太累了, 我们别去看电影了。

　　 B: _____

(2) A: 我天不怕、地不怕, 树林里几只老虎算什么?

　　 B: _____

7　……胜过…… (to hang over; to appear much more prominent or important than . . .)

(1) 现在的中国, 冷漠之气胜过了有修养的文化气氛。
(In today's China, an air of indifference hangs over the refined cultural atmosphere.)

(2) 春天草绿花开, 我喜欢春天胜过夏天或是秋天。
(In the spring, the grass turns green and the flowers start to bloom. I like spring more than summer or autumn.)

(3) 行动胜过空谈。
(Actions speak louder than empty words.)

用 "……胜过……" 完成句子:

(1) 我爱任何人不会胜过

_____

(2) 在中文方面, 我的听力胜过

_____

练习

一. 根据课文, 回答问题

(1) 制度可以解决社会问题吗? 法律可以阻止违规吗?
(2) "法令滋彰, 盗贼多有" 是什么意思?
(3) 与中国相比, 欧美社会的秩序怎么样?
(4) 信仰有助于社会秩序的建立和维护吗?

二. 至少用三个新词语回答以下每个问题, 请在每个新词语下面划出一道线

(1) 你在中国看到哪些不遵守法律法规的现象?
(2) 你认为应该怎么解决人们随地吐痰的问题?
(3) 一个地方的犯罪率或高或低, 跟什么有关系?
(4) 为什么北美市场比较规范、讲诚信?

三. 写作练习

题目:《法律与道德》字数: 500–700字。
　　　下笔以前, 请考虑以下方面:

(1) 现代社会有哪些行为是被法律允许却会受到道德谴责的? 有哪些行为被法律禁止但道德却认同?
(2) 法律解决了哪些社会问题? 是如何解决的? 道德呢?
(3) 法律如何在现实与心理方面发挥作用? 道德呢?

四. 讨论

(1) 有没有绝对公平的制度? 请尝试设计一个最简单的绝对公平的制度, 让全班人都找不出不公平的地方。
(2) 本市的公交系统有什么不完善的地方? 请提出你的改进方案。
(3) 据你的观察和体验, 本校的制度有没有缺陷? 如果有, 为什么这个缺陷会存在? 应该怎么改革? 改革的阻力是什么? 可以克服吗? 怎么克服?
(4) 请在中文网站上找一篇文章, 介绍一下中国政府或者一个地方政府改革的经历。

五. 辩论

题目:约束人们行为的两种准则, 一是法律, 二是道德。法律重要还是道德重要?
正方:法律比道德重要
反方:道德比法律重要
辩论内容可以考虑以下方面:

(1) 你同意"法律是道德的底线、道德的保障"吗?
(2) "法律是外化的, 道德是内化的"吗?
(3) 法律是否都公平? 人的道德标准是否都一致?
(4) 触犯法律与触犯道德底线是否会受到谴责和惩罚?
(5) 我们需要法律禁止以及惩罚不道德的行为, 我们是否也需要法律褒奖以及支持高尚的道德行为?

第二单元

喜与忧

第3课　大过年的烦心事

Figure 3.1 去谁家过年争执不休
by Mingming Cheung (2020)

© Mingming Cheung.

Figure 3.2 今年去婆婆家, 明年去丈母娘家
by Mingming Cheung (2020)

© Mingming Cheung.

Figure 3.3 4+2+1法: 四个老人小两口再带上
孩子一起过年
by Mingming Cheung (2020)

© Mingming Cheung.

Figure 3.4 除夕晚上先去一方家, 再去另外一家
by Mingming Cheung (2020)

© Mingming Cheung.

　　春节是一家团圆的时刻，但是对于中国有些年轻夫妻来说，到谁家去过年却是个很头痛的事情。就回家过年这个问题，记者采访了两对年轻伴侣。

　　王莉和李锋这对小夫妻今年就再次因为到底去谁家过年而争执不休。王莉家在重庆，李锋家在武汉，两人都是独生子女，两边的父母都想让他们到自己家过年，这就难为了小两口。王莉表示，每年临近春节，两人就开始讨论到哪里过年。以前他们还会争吵，现在两人都觉得应该照顾到双方的父母。因此从今年起，他们决定轮流在各自的父母家里过年。李锋告诉记者，今年总算把到谁家过年这个头痛的问题解决了。

　　但是对于恋人陈旭日和王秀丽来说，今年却因为回谁家过年两人意见不一，差点导致两人分道扬镳。几日以前，在重庆上班的陈旭日接到母亲从四川宜宾打来的电话，母亲要求他和女朋友今年一起回家过年，并说已经备好了年货。考虑到自己常年在外，很少陪父母，因此陈旭日就打电话与女友商量，要求她到宜宾过年。但是家住重庆的王秀丽也是家里的独生女，父母当然希望她在家过年。因为如果她不在，就会剩下她的父母两人。王秀丽接到陈旭日的电话后立刻表示，她不能陪他到宜宾过年。陈旭日听了很生气。他觉得，平时他们都在重庆，经常到女朋友家去，过年了，应该照顾一下他的父母，到他家里过年。两人在电话上争吵起来，最后大家都赌气，说干脆就断绝关系。事后陈旭日很后悔，两人大学就开始谈恋爱，彼此相爱已经五年了，如今就因为到谁家过年谈不拢而分手，实在有点不值得。过了一段时间，他打电话给女友让她谅解。王秀丽其实也很后悔，两人说定今年还是和往年一样，在各自父母家里过年。

　　中国自从 1982 年 9 月正式实行计划生育政策，至今已经有 30 多年了。现在中国的年轻夫妇几乎清一色是独生子女。记者在采访中发现，春节夫妻双方去谁家过的确是个问题，其中除夕更是争论焦点，不少人都有何去何从的两难选择和选择后的郁闷。

　　一些受访的在外打工的年轻夫妇告诉记者，到谁家过年确实给在外打工一族带来很大困扰。两家离得很远的夫妻，一个天南，一个地北。坐火车吧，票难买，一个假期不够两人来回跑路；乘飞机吧，价格又太高，年终奖可能都要用去大半。现在的家庭都是一个孩子，一对夫妻上面有四位老人，到时无论跟哪一家过年，另一家必定是冷清的。

　　就去谁家过年这个头痛的事，四川省社科院的胡光伟副所长给年轻夫妇们提出以下几种解决方案：

轮流坐庄法：今年去婆婆家，明年去丈母娘家，这种方法的"公平"可谓显而易见。

　　4+2+1 法: 所谓 4+2+1, 就是四个老人、小两口再带上孩子一起过年。把双方的老爸老妈凑到一起过年, 人多热闹。

　　"赶场" 法: 除夕晚上先去一方家, 再去另外一方家。这个方法比较累, 而且要求夫妻双方家相距不能太远。

　　各归各位法: 双方都怕自己老爸、老妈过年寂寞, 那就只好牺牲一下二人世界, 各回各家。

　　自我调节法: 春节在谁家过了, 这一年的黄金周就去另外一家过。

　　回家的选择虽说很多, 然而有一点却是共同的: 过年, 决不能因为怒气影响到欢庆。

(选自海阔天空的博客文章 "独生子女夫妻该去谁家过年",
2008年2月9日, 有删改 http://blog.sina.com.cn/s/blog_
509aee5a01008jxd.html)

第3課　大過年的煩心事

　　春節是一家團圓的時刻, 但是對于中國有些年輕夫妻來說, 到誰家去過年卻是個很頭痛的事情。就回家過年這個問題, 記者采訪了兩對年輕伴侶。

　　王莉和李鋒這對小夫妻今年就再次因為到底去誰家過年而爭執不休。王莉家在重慶, 李鋒家在武漢, 兩人都是獨生子女, 兩邊的父母都想讓他們到自己家過年, 這就難為了小兩口。王莉表示, 每年臨近春節, 兩人就開始討論到哪裏過年。以前他們還會爭吵, 現在兩人都覺得應該照顧到雙方的父母。因此從今年起, 他們決定輪流在各自的父母家裡過年。李鋒告訴記者, 今年總算把到誰家過年這個頭痛的問題解決了。

　　但是對于戀人陳旭日和王秀麗來說, 今年卻因為回誰家過年兩人意見不一, 差點導致兩人分道揚鑣。幾日以前, 在重慶上班的陳旭日接到母親從四川宜賓打來的電話, 母親要求他和女朋友今年一起回家過年, 並說已經備好了年貨。考慮到自己常年在外, 很少陪父母, 因此陳旭日就打電話與女友商量, 要求她到宜賓過年。但是家住重慶的王秀麗也是家裏的獨生女, 父母當然希望她在家過年。因為如果她不在, 就會剩下她的父母兩人。王秀麗接到陳旭日的電話後立刻表示, 她不能陪他到宜賓過年。陳旭日聽了很生氣。他覺得, 平時他們都在重慶, 經常到女朋友家去, 過年了, 應該照顧一下他的父母, 到他家裡過年。兩人在電話上爭吵起來, 最後大家都賭氣, 說乾脆就斷絕關係。事後陳旭日很後悔, 兩人大學就開始談戀愛, 彼此相愛已經五年了, 如今就因為到誰家過年談不攏而分手, 實在有點不值得。過了一段時間, 他打電話給女友讓她諒解。王秀麗其實也很後悔,兩人說定今年還是和往年一樣,在各自父母家裏過年。

中國自從1982年9月正式實行計劃生育政策,至今已經有30多年了。現在中國的年輕夫婦幾乎清一色是獨生子女。記者在采訪中發現,春節夫妻雙方去誰家過的確是個問題,其中除夕更是爭論焦點,不少人都有何去何從的兩難選擇和選擇後的鬱悶。

一些受訪的在外打工的年輕夫婦告訴記者,到誰家過年確實給在外打工一族帶來很大困擾。兩家離得很遠的夫妻,一個天南,一個地北。坐火車吧,票難買,一個假期不夠兩人來回跑路;乘飛機吧,價格又太高,年終獎可能都要用去大半。現在的家庭都是一個孩子,一對夫妻上面有四位老人,到時無論跟哪一家過年,另一家必定是冷清的。

就去誰家過年這個頭痛的事,四川省社科院的胡光偉副所長給年輕夫婦們提出以下幾種解決方案:

輪流坐莊法:今年去婆婆家,明年去丈母娘家,這種方法的“公平”可謂顯而易見。

4+2+1法:所謂4+2+1,就是四個老人、小兩口再帶上孩子一起過年。把雙方的老爸老媽凑到一起過年,人多熱鬧。

“趕場”法:除夕晚上先去一方家,再去另外一方家。這個方法比較累,而且要求夫妻雙方家相距不能太遠。

各歸各位法:雙方都怕自己老爸、老媽過年寂寞,那就只好犧牲一下二人世界,各回各家。

自我調節法:春節在誰家過了,這一年的黃金周就去另外一家過。

回家的選擇雖說很多,然而有一點卻是共同的:過年,決不能因為怒氣影響到歡慶。

(选自海阔天空的博客文章“独生子女夫妻该去谁家过年”,2008年2月9日,有删改 http://blog.sina.com.cn/s/blog_509aee5a01008jxd.html)

新词语

烦心	煩心	fánxīn	annoyed 那孩子真淘气,让人~/别~,我请你吃饭
团圆	團圓	tuányuán	(family) reunion 全家~/~饭
时刻	時刻	shíkè	(a point in) time; moment 重要~/最开心的~
采访	採訪	cǎifǎng	to have an interview with; interview 记者在~运动员/他接受了记者的~
伴侣	伴侶	bànlǚ	partners 终身~/~关系
难为	難為	nánwéi	to put pressure on somebody; to make things difficult for somebody 他不会唱歌,你们就别~他了/我不是有心~你

临近	臨近	línjìn	to be close to in time; 在时间上紧接靠近 ~节日/~考试
不一	不一	bùyī	different; not the same; 不同 观点~/观众反应~
导致	導致	dǎozhì	to lead to; to result in 那件事故~40多人伤亡/他的不努力会~他的失败
年货	年貨	niánhuò	special goods for the Spring Festival 商店都在进~/我在商场办~
常年	常年	chángnián	all year round; year in and year out 他~不回家/那间咖啡馆生意~都很好
剩下	剩下	shèngxià	to be left behind; to be left over 父母都在外打工, 只~孩子在家/这个月我们就~两块钱
赌气	賭氣	dǔqì	to feel wronged and then act rashly; to act willfully or in a fit of pique; 觉得被误解很生气 那孩子~不吃饭/他~走了
断绝	斷絕	duànjué	to break off; to sever ~联系/~往来
后悔	後悔	hòuhuǐ	to regret ~做错事/有一天会~的
谈不拢	談不攏	tánbùlǒng	unable to reach an agreement; 谈不到一起 房子没买成, 我们跟房主价钱~/他们夫妻问题太多, 老是~
值得	值得	zhídé	to be worth 不~生气/那个地方很~去
谅解	諒解	liàngjiě	to understand after learning the truth; understanding; 原谅、理解 希望你能~我/请~孩子的无知/得到大家的~/感谢你的~
争论	爭論	zhēnglùn	debate; to debate 一场~/~一个学术问题
焦点	焦點	jiāodiǎn	focus ~放在经济上/成为关注的~
何去何从	何去何從	hé qù hé cóng	what course to follow; what decision to make; 去: 抛去; 从: 选择; 不知怎么办 没考上大学的他不知道~/在这重要时刻, 他不知~
两难	兩難	liǎngnán	to face a dilemma 进退~/面临~的选择
郁闷	鬱悶	yùmèn	gloom; depression; gloomy; depressed 消除心中的~/失业后的~/心情~/感到~
受访	受訪	shòufǎng	to be interviewed; 受: 接受; 访:采访 ~的对象/~的学生
困扰	困擾	kùnrǎo	confusion; perplexed 他陷于~之中/这个问题让她很~
天南地北	天南地北	tiān nán dì běi	far apart; places far from each other; 相距遥远 来自~的年轻人很快成了朋友
年终奖	年終獎	niánzhōngjiǎng	year-end bonus 发~/领~
冷清	冷清	lěngqīng	empty and deserted 那个小城的街道晚上很~/公园游客很少, 很~
社科院	社科院	Shèkēyuàn	Academy of Social Sciences; 社会科学研究院
副	副	fù	assistant; vice; deputy ~教授/~总统/~主任
轮流坐庄	輪流坐莊	lúnliú zuòzhuāng	to take turns being the dealer in mahjong; to take turns being the person in charge 打麻将时, 四人~/主席这一位置由他们三个人~
婆婆	婆婆	pópo	husband's mother 公公~

丈母娘	丈母娘	zhàngmuniáng	wife's mother 丈人~
可谓	可謂	kěwèi	it may be said; 可以说 他对朋友~尽心尽力/他的爱情~来得快也去得快
显而易见	顯而易見	xiǎn ér yì jiàn	obvious; apparently 他的优点~/~, 他没听懂意思
凑	湊	còu	to gather together; 聚合 朋友常常~在一起吃饭、聊天/他生病住院了, 同学们~钱帮助他
赶场	趕場	gǎnchǎng	(of an actor) to hurry from one place to another to perform; 演员去一个地方表演完毕以后赶紧到另一个地方去表演 他一次次~, 很累/有些父母像~一样送孩子去学这学那
相距	相距	xiāngjù	to be separated by (a certain distance or a period of time) 两地~50里/他们出生年代~十年
牺牲	犧牲	xīshēng	to sacrifice 他~休息时间帮助我/为了成功, 他~了幸福
调节	調節	tiáojié	to adjust ~室内温度/~座椅的高度
黄金周	黃金周	huángjīnzhōu	Golden Week 春节~/十一~

重点词语和句式

1 就……问题 (regarding or about [an issue or question])

(1) 就回家过年这个问题, 记者采访了两对年轻伴侣。
(Regarding the issue of returning home to celebrate the Spring Festival, the reporter interviewed two young couples.)

(2) 就经济合作问题, 双方代表进行了讨论。
(On the question of economic cooperation, representatives of both sides joined in a discussion.)

(3) 就环境问题, 记者采访了北京市市长。
(The reporter interviewed the mayor of Beijing about environmental issues.)

翻译:

(1) I haven't gotten a raise in three years. I would like to discuss the issue of my salary with my boss.

_____

(2) The two teachers often consult each other on the question of how best to teach students.

_____

2 差点 (chàdiǎn almost; nearly)

(1) 因为回谁家过年两人意见不一, 差点导致两人分道扬镳。
(Because they disagreed on which home to return to for the Spring Festival, they almost parted and went their separate ways.)

(2) 今早我起床太晚, 差点上课迟到。
(I got out of bed too late this morning. I was almost late for class.)

(3) 下雪天, 路滑, 我差点摔了一跤。
(It was a snowy day. The streets were slippery. I nearly fell.)

翻译:

(1) I forgot to prepare for today's quiz; I almost flunked it.

_____

(2) My goodness! That car nearly hit us.

_____

3　分道扬镳 (*fēn dào yáng biāo* to part and go separate ways)

(1) 因为回谁家过年两人意见不一, 差点导致两人分道扬镳。
(Because they disagreed on which home to return to for the Spring Festival, they almost parted and went their separate ways.)

(2) 因为政治观点不同, 他们分道扬镳。
(Because they differed in their political views, they parted and went their separate ways.)

(3) 有些夫妻生活多年以后分道扬镳。
(Some husbands and wives part and go their separate ways after living together for many years.)

翻译:

(1) The tennis star and her coach did not get along. They parted and went their separate ways.

_____

(2) If you don't love me anymore, let's part and go our separate ways.

_____

4　考虑到 (considering that; considering something; to take into consideration)

(1) 考虑到自己常年在外, 很少陪父母, ⋯⋯ [他]要求她到宜宾过年。
(Considering that he had been away from home for many years and had rarely spent time with his parents, . . . he asked her to go to Yibin for the New Year.)

(2) 考虑到他的年龄, 能跑完马拉松已经很不错了。
(Considering his age, it was pretty amazing that he was able to finish the marathon.)

(3) 女孩跟男友私奔了, 她完全没有考虑到父母的感受。
(The girl eloped with her boyfriend. She didn't take her parents' feelings into consideration at all.)

用"考虑到"完成句子:

(1) 考虑到 _____, 我决定不买汽车。

(2) 他们考虑到他_____, 决定不麻烦他帮忙了。

5　干脆 (might as well; simply)

(1) 两人在电话上争吵起来, 最后两人赌气, 说干脆就断绝关系。
(They argued over the phone. Afterwards, they were both piqued and decided that they might as well break up.)

(2) 别拉长脸坐在那儿, 你不高兴, 干脆说出来。
(Don't just sit there with a long face. If you are unhappy, you might as well say why.)

(3) 虽然我们说好去看电影, 要是你太累, 干脆别去了。
(Although we already agreed to go to the movies, if you are too tired to go, we can simply call it off.)

用"干脆"完成句子:

(1) 既然做饭那么麻烦, 干脆 _____

(2) 是你打碎了花瓶吧, 别装了, 干脆 _____

6　清一色 (all; exclusively; literally, of the same color)

(1) 现在中国的年轻人几乎清一色是独生子女。
(Nowadays young people in China are almost all only children.)

(2) 我喜欢穿黑色, 我的衣服几乎清一色是黑色。
(I like to wear black. My clothes are almost exclusively black.)

(3) 这个饭馆汉堡包好吃, 客人几乎清一色都是年轻人。
(This restaurant has delicious hamburgers. Its customers are almost exclusively young people.)

翻译:

(1) The Chicago Bulls (*Zhījiāgē Gōngniú* 芝加哥公牛) basketball team wears all-red uniforms.

_____

(2) The engineering conference attendees were almost exclusively men.

_____

7　A 吧, ……, B 吧, …… (option A, . . ., option B, . . .)

(1) 坐火车吧, 票难买, 一个假期不够两人来回跑路; 乘飞机吧, 价格又太高, 年终奖可能都要用去大半。
(If we decided to take the train, we would have trouble buying tickets. [Also,] one week's holiday wouldn't be long enough for us to travel there and back. If we flew, it would cost too much. Most of our year-end bonuses would probably be used up.)

(2) 到了"十一"黄金周, 我们陷入了两难的选择: 出去旅游吧, 人太多; 呆在家里吧, 没有意思。
(As the October 1st Golden Week approached, we were faced with a dilemma. If we traveled, we would run into crowds. If we stayed home, we would be bored.)

(3) 我们应该吃有机食品吗? 吃吧, 也许对身体比较好; 不吃吧, 能省点儿钱。
(Should we eat organic food? If we did, we would probably be healthier. If we didn't, we would be able to save a little money.)

用 "A 吧, ……, B 吧, ……" 完成对话:

(1) A: 你想当医生还是音乐家?

　　 B: _____

(2) A: 你们买还是不买那座房子?

　　 B: _____

8　所谓……就是…… (the so-called . . . is; the term or expression . . . refers to)

(1) 所谓 4+2+1, 就是四个老人、小两口再带上孩子一起过年。
(The so-called "4+2+1" [solution] is for four elderly people, a young couple, and a child to celebrate the New Year together.)

(2) 所谓 "蓝领工人" 就是做体力劳动的人。
(The term "blue-collar worker" refers to someone who performs manual labor.)

(3) 所谓活字典就是一个知识渊博的人。
(The expression "a walking dictionary" refers to a person who has broad, scholarly knowledge.)

用 "所谓……就是……" 完成句子:

(1) 所谓 "赶场法", 就是_____

(2) 所谓 "各归各位" 法, 就是_____

9　决不 (definitely not 一定不)

(1) 过年, 决不能因为怒气影响到欢庆。
(During the Chinese New Year, we definitely shouldn't let anger get in the way of our celebration.)

(2) 就是工作再辛苦, 我也决不会抱怨。
(No matter how hard I have to work, I will definitely not complain.)

(3) 有的女人认为决不应该告诉别人自己的年龄。
(Some women think that they should definitely not let other people know their ages.)

用 "决不" 完成句子:

(1) A: 你都三十好几了, 你打算结婚吗?

　　 B: _____

(2) A: 你的孩子常吃炸鸡、炸薯条吗?

　　 B: _____

练习

一. 根据课文，回答问题

(1) 课文里的年轻夫妻、恋人面临什么样的问题？
(2) 是哪些原因造成了年轻伴侣回家过年的问题？
(3) 四川省社科院的胡光伟副所长给出什么样的解决方案？
(4) 在北美，大家在谁家过节？安排在这家过节时有没有让人头痛的问题？

二. 至少用三个新词语完成以下每段对话，请在新词语下面划出一道线

(1) A: 听说小红跟她的男朋友分道扬镳了，这是怎么一回事？

　　B: _____

(2) A: 你们夫妻俩今年过年打算去谁家啊？

　　B: _____

(3) A: 我父母让我们去上海过年，她父母让我们今年去北京过年。为这事，我们俩争论了好几天了。你有什么好主意？

　　B: _____

三. 写作练习

你是一个记者，采访了几对年轻夫妻和恋人，请他们谈谈春节有没有什么让他们很烦恼的事，然后写一篇文章。题目自己决定，字数: 500–700 字。

四. 讨论

(1) 以前中国的年轻夫妻有没有类似的烦恼？为什么？
(2) 2016年1月起中国全面实施二孩政策，以后中国的年轻夫妻还会有类似的烦恼吗？为什么？
(3) 北美的年轻夫妻有没有类似的烦恼？为什么？
(4) 中国、西方对父母与子女关系看法是否相同？
(5) 请你在网络上找一个与本课话题有关系的故事，讨论时讲给大家听。

五. 辩论

题目: 年轻夫妻应该回谁家过年？
正方: 年轻夫妻应该一起回夫家或是妻家过年
反方: 年轻夫妻应该各自回家过年
辩论内容可以考虑以下方面:

(1) 依照中国传统，夫妻应该去谁家过年？
(2) 要是夫妻两家都在本地或是两家都在外地，他们应该回谁家过年？
(3) 要是夫妻一家在本地、一家在外地，他们应该在本地还是外地过年？
(4) 要是夫妻各自回家过年，孩子应该跟谁？

第4课 大学生竞聘搓澡工、淘粪工、环卫工，是喜还是忧？

Figure 4.1 洗浴中心招聘
by Mingming Cheung (2020)

© Mingming Cheung.

Figure 4.2 招聘5名淘粪工
by Mingming Cheung (2020)

© Mingming Cheung.

Figure 4.3 大学生在家当啃老族
by Mingming Cheung (2020)

© Mingming Cheung.

Figure 4.4 上学苦
by Mingming Cheung (2020)

© Mingming Cheung.

2007年,北京一家洗浴中心招聘管理人员和搓澡工,注明所有职位均要求大专以上学历。出人意料的是,招聘现场吸引了近百名大学生。搓澡工一向被认为是低等工作,为什么有那么多受过高等教育的大学生会去应聘?洗浴中心负责人介绍,此次不管是管理岗位还是基层工作,都要从搓澡、捏脚等底层服务做起。除了来到现场的应聘者,洗浴中心还收到了5000多名大学生的申请,其中2000名大学生应聘搓澡工职位。

大学生竞聘低等职位的工作似乎已经成了普遍现象,类似的情况数不胜数。2010年,山东济南招聘5名淘粪工,最终拿到工作的竟然全是大学生。这些大学生需要通过半年试用期,才能与用人单位正式签订合同,成为有资格正式上岗的淘粪工。2012年,哈尔滨招聘457个环卫工,一共引来了11539个报名者。进入最终竞争的7186人中,约3000人拥有本科学历,还有29名硕士生。

搓澡、捏脚、淘粪、清扫街道,看似与大学生的身份风马牛不相及,但是这样的职位却吸引了众多天之骄子争相应聘,难怪会引发人们的热议,叫好的人有之,感到痛惜的人有之。

有人分析说,中国大学1990年以前实行的是精英教育,高考录取仅有30%左右,从100人中筛选出来的30人可以说是顶尖人才。那时的大学生毕业后相当抢手,不但能找到工作,而且无论是地位还是待遇都是没有受过高等教育的人没法比的。可是近年来,随着大学的年年扩招,北京等一些地方的录取率几乎达到了80%以上,大学生已经不再是什么稀罕物了。每年几百万的大学毕业生涌入社会,就业市场的吸收能力却远远赶不上逐年递增的就业大军;再加上不少拥有高学历的学子对工作的期望很高,非高工资的单位不去,非大城市不去,这种高不成低不就的择业观让他们处处碰壁。

现在,大学生就业问题成为上至政府官员下至普通百姓关注的焦点。在这种情况下,不少人认为,竞聘搓澡工、淘粪工、环卫工的大学生们放下身段,降低条件,选择一份看似不体面的工作,解决自己的生存问题,无疑是一种理性的选择;这总比找不到工作,在家当"啃老族"强吧。所以说,这些大学生勇于改变就业观,抛弃贵贱观念,勤奋自强,脚踏实地,从低等职位做起,实在值得喝彩。

另一种截然相反的看法是,本来初中毕业生就能干的活让大学生来干,是大材小用、是浪费人才。中国还是发展中国家,需要人才的地方多的是,还没有发达到当个搓澡工、淘粪工、环卫工也得有高学历的地步。新闻报道里总是说多少大学生毕业后找不到工作,难道中国的大学生真的过剩了吗?绝对不是!就目前来说,在相对贫穷落后的广大农村乡镇,特别是西部地区,不知道有多么渴求专业人才，而大学生们却扎堆去应聘北京的搓澡工。他们宁可学非所用，留在北京当搓澡工，也不愿意去迫切需要人才的西部当公务员和教师。

对学生本人来说，读了十四、五年的书，先不说经济成本，只说无数次的考试，无数个夜晚的挑灯夜战，结果就是为了成为一名搓澡工或是淘粪工，这难道不让人寒心吗？当初父母逼着孩子放弃兴趣爱好，放弃快乐和自由，去取得那一纸好分数，决不会是为了让孩子去做一名环卫工吧！是的，职业本无贵贱之分，但是成为熟练甚至优秀的搓澡工、淘粪工或是环卫工需要接受十四、五年的教育吗？技校毕业生或经过短期培训的人员难道不能胜任这样的工作吗？这些大学生去当搓澡工、淘粪工、环卫工不是浪费人才、荒废学业是什么？这些招聘的企业是拿大学生开涮，不需要高学历的职位，却要抬高门槛，非大学生不要，这不仅是侮辱大学生，也是对知识的轻蔑。

大学生竞聘搓澡工、淘粪工、环卫工，我们应该是喜还是忧？

第4課　大學生競聘搓澡工、淘糞工、環衛工，是喜還是憂？

2007年，北京一家洗浴中心招聘管理人員和搓澡工，註明所有職位均要求大專以上學歷。出人意料的是，招聘現場吸引了近百名大學生。搓澡工一向被認為是低等工作，為什麼有那麼多受過高等教育的大學生會去應聘？洗浴中心負責人介紹，此次不管是管理崗位還是基層工作，都要從搓澡、捏腳等底層服務做起。除了來到現場的應聘者，洗浴中心還收到了5000多名大學生的申請，其中2000名大學生應聘搓澡工職位。

大學生競聘低等職位的工作似乎已經成了普遍現象，類似的情況數不勝數。2010年，山東濟南招聘5名淘糞工，最終拿到工作的竟然全是大學生。這些大學生需要通過半年試用期，才能與用人單位正式簽訂合同，成為有資格正式上崗的淘糞工。2012年，哈爾濱招聘457個環衛工，一共引來了11539個報名者。進入最終競爭的7186人中，約3000人擁有本科學歷，還有29名碩士生。

搓澡、捏腳、淘糞、清掃街道，看似與大學生的身份風馬牛不相及，但是這樣的職位卻吸引了眾多天之驕子爭相應聘，難怪會引發人們的熱議，叫好的人有之，感到痛惜的人有之。

有人分析說，中國大學1990年以前實行的是精英教育，高考錄取僅有30%左右，從100人中篩選出來的30人可以說是頂尖人才。那時的大學生畢業後相當搶手，不但能找到工作，而且無論是地位還是待遇都是沒有受過高等教育的人沒法比的。可是近年來，隨著大學的年年擴招，北京等一些地方的錄取率幾乎達到了

80%以上, 大學生已經不再是什麼稀罕物了。每年幾百萬的大學畢業生涌入社會, 就業市場的吸收能力卻遠遠趕不上逐年遞增的就業大軍; 再加上不少擁有高學歷的學子對工作的期望很高, 非高工資的單位不去, 非大城市不去, 這種高不成低不就的擇業觀讓他們處處碰壁。

現在, 大學生就業問題成為上至政府官員下至普通百姓關注的焦點。在這種情況下, 不少人認為, 競聘搓澡工、淘糞工、環衛工的大學生們放下身段, 降低條件, 選擇一份看似不體面的工作, 解決自己的生存問題, 無疑是一種理性的選擇; 這總比找不到工作, 在家當"啃老族"強吧。所以說, 這些大學生勇於改變就業觀, 拋棄貴賤觀念, 勤奮自強, 腳踏實地, 從低等職位做起, 實在值得喝彩。

另一種截然相反的看法是, 本來初中畢業生就能幹的活讓大學生來幹, 是大材小用、是浪費人才。中國還是發展中國家, 需要人才的地方多的是, 還沒有發達到當個搓澡工、淘糞工、環衛工也得有高學歷的地步。新聞報道裏總是說多少大學生畢業後找不到工作, 難道中國的大學生真的過剩了嗎? 絕對不是! 就目前來說, 在相對貧窮落後的廣大農村鄉鎮, 特別是西部地區, 不知道有多麼渴求專業人才, 而大學生們卻紮堆去應聘北京的搓澡工。他們寧可學非所用, 留在北京當搓澡工, 也不願意去迫切需要人才的西部當公務員和教師。

對學生本人來說, 讀了十四、五年的書, 先不說經濟成本, 只說無數次的考試, 無數個夜晚的挑燈夜戰, 結果就是為了成為一名搓澡工或是淘糞工, 這難道不讓人寒心嗎? 當初父母逼著孩子放棄興趣愛好, 放棄快樂和自由, 去取得那一紙好分數, 決不會是為了讓孩子去做一名環衛工吧! 是的, 職業本無貴賤之分, 但是成為熟練甚至優秀的搓澡工、淘糞工或是環衛工需要接受十四、五年的教育嗎? 技校畢業生或經過短期培訓的人員難道不能勝任這樣的工作嗎? 這些大學生去當搓澡工、淘糞工、環衛工不是浪費人才、荒廢學業是什麼? 這些招聘的企業是拿大學生開涮, 不需要高學歷的職位, 卻要擡高門檻, 非大學生不要, 這不僅是侮辱大學生, 也是對知識的輕蔑。

大學生競聘搓澡工、淘糞工、環衛工, 我們應該是喜還是憂?

新词语

竞聘	競聘	jìngpìn	to compete to be hired; 竞: 竞争; 聘: 应聘 ~上岗/~成功
搓澡	搓澡	cuōzǎo	to give someone a rubdown with a damp towel; to scrub and wash; 搓: 擦 ~工/给客人~

淘粪	淘糞	táofèn	to scoop human excrement out of a cesspit; 淘: 从深处挖出脏物 在粪池~/以~为生
环卫工	環衛工	huánwèigōng	sanitation worker (包括清洁路面、公厕和垃圾站) 关心~群体/~的工作
洗浴	洗浴	xǐyù	to bathe ~用品/~盆
出人意料	出人意料	chū rén yì liào	unexpected; to come as a surprise; 超乎人们的预料 这个结果~/~的消息
应聘	應聘	yìngpìn	to apply for a job vacancy ~售货员的工作/~者
捏脚	捏腳	niējiǎo	to massage the foot ~器; 捏: 1. 用拇指和其他手指夹住 捏肩/捏背 2. 用手指把软的东西做成一定的形状 捏饺子/捏面人
底层	底層	dǐcéng	bottom layer; ground floor 社会~/一套在~的公寓
试用期	試用期	shìyòngqī	probation period; 用一个人一段时期，看看这个人适合不适合这份工作 三个月的~/他已完成~，成为正式员工
签订	簽訂	qiāndìng	to sign a contract or an agreement; 订立合同或是条约并且签字 ~合约/~协定
合同	合同	hétóng	contract 签一张~/终止~
看似	看似	kànsì	to seem; 看起来像 ~简单其实复杂/~无情却有情
身份	身份	shēnfèn	position; identity 以妻子的~要求继承丈夫遗产/真实~
风马牛不相及	風馬牛不相及	fēng mǎ niú bù xiāng jí	to have absolutely nothing in common with each other; 完全没有共同处; 风: 走失; 及: 到; 来自《左传》(The Zuo Commentary covers the history of the period 722–468 BC), 本指齐国、楚国离得很远，即使马牛走失，也不会跑到对方的境内 这两件事~，不能混为一谈/别怪他，他和这件事~/我问她今天天气，她说想吃糖，真是~/他不能回答问题，说了一些~的话
天之骄子	天之驕子	tiān zhī jiāo zǐ	child of fortune; exceptionally privileged person; 汉朝 (202 BC–220 AD) 时，匈奴自称为"天之骄子"，意思是匈奴为老天所宠爱 她一夜成名，可以说是~/在中国大学生被称为~
热议	熱議	rèyì	heated debate; to debate heatedly 引发公众的~/近来网民~炒股
叫好	叫好	jiàohǎo	to applaud; to shout "bravo"; 喊好表示赞赏 鼓掌~/观众叫起好来
痛惜	痛惜	tòngxī	to feel deep regret; 心痛惋惜 ~他的不幸
精英	精英	jīngyīng	outstanding person; elite 社会~/~阶层 (jiēcéng class)
筛选	篩選	shāixuǎn	to separate the wheat from the chaff; sifting; 去掉不需要的，留下需要的 不合格的人被~掉了/经过反复~，选出两人
顶尖	頂尖	dǐngjiān	outstanding; extraordinary; 最优秀的 ~运动员/他人才、相貌都是~的
扩招	擴招	kuòzhāo	to increase student enrollment numbers; 扩大招生 大学~两千人

录取率	錄取率	lùqǔlǜ	acceptance rate 大学~上升/申请~下降
稀罕物	稀罕物	xīhǎnwù	rarity 这种水果在北方是~/北京的胡同逐渐成了~
涌入	涌入	yǒngrù	to swarm into; 涌: 水从下向上冒出来, 形容像水冒出来 大量游客~城市/难民不断~欧洲
逐年	逐年	zhúnián	year after year 收入~增加/出生率~降低
递增	遞增	dìzēng	to grow or increase gradually; 一次次增加 人口~/产量~
就业大军	就業大軍	jiùyè dàjūn	workforce 涌入~/加入~
高不成低不就	高不成低不就	gāo bù chéng dī bú jiù	unable to have the best but unwilling to settle for less 大学毕业以后, ~, 他老没工作/这个老姑娘~, 到今天还没结婚
碰壁	碰壁	pèngbì	to hit a wall; 遭遇挫折 找工作~/在父母那里碰了壁
放下身段	放下身段	fàngxià shēnduàn	to humble oneself; with humility 放下架子 有时候要出头必须~/大学生就业要~
体面	體面	tǐmiàn	respectable; decent ~的生活/不~的行为
无疑	無疑	wúyí	undoubtedly; 毫无疑问 她~是我最好的朋友/他找女朋友~要求很高
理性	理性	lǐxìng	rational; rationally; rationality ~的决定/~对待/失去~; 反义词: 感性
啃老族	啃老族	kěnlǎozú	adult children who live off their parents; 啃: 一点点咬下来 啃骨头/啃玉米; 有些失业青年成为~/他们长期依赖父母, 是标准的~
抛弃	拋棄	pāoqì	to abandon ~坏习惯/被人~
贵贱	貴賤	guìjiàn	noble and base; 贵: 地位很高; 贱: 地位很低 人无~/职业不分~
自强	自強	zìqiáng	to strengthen oneself; self improvement; 自己奋发努力 我们要~/自信、~是她的特征
脚踏实地	腳踏實地	jiǎo tà shí dì	down-to-earth; to have both feet on the ground; 比喻做事踏实、认真 他是个~的人/做人要~
喝彩	喝彩	hècǎi	to cheer; 大声叫好 大家都为钢琴家~/观众又是~, 又是鼓掌
截然相反	截然相反	jié rán xiāng fǎn	completely different 实际情况跟我们想的~/他们对问题的看法~
大材小用	大材小用	dà cái xiǎo yòng	to waste one's great talent on an insignificant job; underemployed; 把大的材料当成小的材料用, 比喻受雇不当, 浪费人才 他是博士, 教小学不是~吗
多的是	多的是	duōdeshì	a lot; 有很多 好人~/她的钱~
过剩	過剩	guòshèng	surplus; excess; 供过于求而剩余 劳动力~/精力~
渴求	渴求	kěqiú	to yearn for ~知识/~别人的理解
宁可	寧可	nìngkě	would rather 我~挨饿也不吃不喜欢的东西/他~穷也不求人
学非所用	學非所用	xué fēi suǒ yòng	a person's occupation has nothing to do with his education 他学的是文学, 却~, 干的是房地产生意

迫切	迫切	pòqiè	urgently; pressing ~希望/~的社会问题
公务员	公務員	gōngwùyuán	civil servant 国家~考试/考~
挑灯夜战	挑燈夜戰	tiǎo dēng yè zhàn	to study or work late into the night; to burn the midnight oil; 挑:翻动;灯:灯芯 (dēngxīn wick); 晚上点着灯读书,形容读书很刻苦 为了完成报告,他~/她~准备考试
寒心	寒心	hánxīn	to be bitterly disappointed; 失望痛心 感到~/让人~
熟练	熟練	shúliàn	skilled 技术~的工人/他是新手, 在工作上, 还不够~
技校	技校	jìxiào	technical school; 技工学校 (中等专业) 上~学习电脑、汽车或是家电维修
培训	培训	péixùn	training; to train; 培养训练 对他们进行~/~教师
胜任	勝任	shèngrèn	to work competently 交给他的工作, 他都能~/这个机器人能~两个工人的工作量
荒废	荒廢	huāngfèi	to waste; deserted ~人生/~的土地
抬高门槛	抬高門檻	táigāo ménkǎn	to raise the standard; 门槛: threshold; 门框下面的横木条或金属条 抬高入学门槛/对申请~
侮辱	侮辱	wǔrǔ	to insult; insult ~女性/这种~
轻蔑	輕蔑	qīngmiè	scorn; scornful; scornfully; 轻视;不屑 表示~/~的语气/~地看着他

重点词语和句式

1　争相 + V (to compete for; to scramble; to vie for)

　　(1) 搓澡、捏脚、淘粪、清扫街道, 看似与大学生的身份风马牛不相及, 但是这样的职位却吸引了众多天之骄子争相应聘。
　　　　(Jobs like giving guests rubdowns with damp cloths, massaging feet, scooping human excrement out of cesspits and sweeping streets all seemed beneath college students, but many privileged young people were competing for them.)

　　(2) 中国经济繁荣, 外国人争相投资。
　　　　(As China's economy booms, foreigners scramble to invest in the country.)

　　(3) 他很优秀, 两家公司争相聘用他。
　　　　(He is outstanding; two companies are vying for him.)

用"争相 + V"完成句子:

　　(1) 新的iPhone一出来, 年轻人 _____

　　(2) 在讨论会上, 学生们 _____

2　……有之, ……有之 (there are . . ., there are [others] . . .; some [people] . . ., others . . .)

　　(1) 但是这样的职位却吸引了众多天之骄子争相应聘, 难怪会引发人们的热议, 叫好的人有之, 感到痛惜的人有之。
　　　　(But such jobs attracted a multitude of college students in competition for them. No wonder the phenomenon touched off such heated debate. There were people who applauded the students; there were others who felt sorry for them.)

(2) 对接受难民, 欢迎者有之, 拒斥者有之。

(When it came to accepting refugees, some people welcomed the idea; others rejected it.)

(3) 对出兵打仗, 支持者有之, 反对者有之。

(When it came to dispatching troops, some people supported the idea; others opposed it.)

用"……有之,……有之"完成对话:

(1) A: 鼓励农民工回乡创业是解决贫困的办法。

　　B: _____

(2) A: 他一夜致富。

　　B: _____

3　抢手 (to be sought after; very popular)

(1) 中国大学1990年以前实行的是精英教育,…… 那时的大学生毕业后相当抢手。

(Before 1990, Chinese universities admitted only the best students. . . . After these students graduated, they were sought after by employers.)

(2) 学商科和理工科的学生在人才市场上很抢手, 学文科的却无人问津。

(Students who study business, science and engineering are very popular in the job market; no one shows any interest in liberal arts students.)

(3) 母亲节什么样的礼物最抢手?

(What kinds of presents are most popular on Mother's Day?)

翻译:

(1) He is a well-known painter. His paintings are sought after by collectors.

_____

(2) The stock market keeps going up. Which stocks are the most popular?

_____

4　非……不…… (absolutely have/has to)

(1) 不少拥有高学历的学子对工作的期望很高, 非高工资的单位不去, 非大城市不去。

(A lot of well-educated students had high job expectations. They absolutely had to work for employers who paid them well; they absolutely had to work in the big cities.)

(2) 有的人很注意健康, 他们非有机食品不吃。

(Some people pay a great deal of attention to their health. They absolutely have to eat organic food.)

(3) 老板很喜欢应聘的年轻人, 他对年轻人说, "我们非你不聘。"

(The boss liked the young man who had applied for the position. He said to him, "We absolutely have to hire you.")

翻译:

(1) She likes to live in luxury. She absolutely has to marry a rich man.

_____

(2) This girl is spoiled. She absolutely has to wear designer clothes.

_____

5 上至……下至…… (from . . . down to . . .)

(1) 大学生就业问题成为上至政府官员下至普通百姓关注的焦点。
(From government officials down to the common people, all focused their attention on the issue of employment for college students.)

(2) 在这家公司，上至老板，下至员工，都很勤奋。
(At this company, everyone works hard, from the boss down to the staff.)

(3) 上至教练，下至队员，都很为打赢这场球赛而兴奋。
(Everyone was excited to win the game, from the coach down to the players.)

用"上至……下至……"完成句子:

(1) 要是人权得不到保障，_____ 都会受到影响。

(2) 这里的古迹 _____

6 总比……强吧 (after all, it would be better than . . .)

(1) 选择一份看似不体面的工作，这总比找不到工作，在家当"啃老族"强吧！
(Opting for a seemingly unprestigious job, after all, would be better than staying unemployed and living off one's parents.)

(2) 面包半个别嫌少，总比没有强吧。
(Half a loaf is, after all, better than none.)

(3) 把烦恼说一说总比憋在心里强吧。
(Expressing your frustrations is, after all, better than bottling them up.)

翻译:

(1) Having an old car is, after all, better than having no car at all.

_____

(2) Being busy is, after all, better than staying idle.

_____

7 扎堆 (zhāduī to crowd together; to huddle together; to join the trend 大家都在一个地方，有凑热闹的意思。)

(1) [那些贫穷、落后的地方]不知道有多么渴求专业人才，而大学生们却扎堆去应聘北京的搓澡工。
([Those poor and backward places] were eager to recruit professionals, but college students crowded together in Beijing to apply for jobs giving guests rubdowns in bathhouses.)

(2) 他们上班时不工作，扎堆聊天。

(While on the job, they didn't work. They huddled together to chat.)

(3) 9月9号那天年轻人扎堆结婚。

(Young people joined the trend of getting married on the 9th of September.)

用"扎堆"完成句子：

(1) 连续几天雾霾，孩子们呼吸道感染，_____

(2) 春节期间大家_____

8 不是A是什么？(What could A be, other than . . . ? If this were not A, what else could it be? What could you call A, if not . . . ?)

(1) 这些大学生去当搓澡工、淘粪工、环卫工不是浪费人才、荒废学业是什么？

(These college students became workers who gave guests rubdowns [in bath-houses], scooped human excrement out of cesspits, and swept streets. What could this have been, other than a waste of talent?)

(2) 我常请他吃饭，他却从不请我吃饭，这不是小气是什么？

(I often invite him for food. He has never invited me back. If this were not stinginess, what else could it be?)

(3) 房东拒绝把房子租给外国人，这不是歧视是什么？

(The landlord refuses to rent to foreigners. What would you call this, if not discrimination?)

翻译：

(1) 这部电影实在愚蠢，不是侮辱我们的智商是什么？

_____

(2) 他生病了还不能休息，这不是老板过分是什么？

_____

9 拿……开涮 (ná . . . kāishuàn to make a fool of somebody; to make fun of somebody; to mock)

(1) 这些招聘的企业是拿大学生开涮，不需要高学历的职位却要抬高门槛非大学生不要。

(These recruiting companies made fools of college graduates. The positions did not need to be filled by highly educated people. Yet the companies raised their standards and would hire only college graduates.)

(2) 他的朋友老拿他开涮，但是他一点儿都不生气。

(His friends often make fun of him, but he doesn't mind at all.)

(3) 美国喜剧演员常拿政治人物开涮。

(American comedians often make fun of politicians.)

用"拿……开涮"完成对话：

(1) A: 你为什么不高兴？

B: _____

(2) A: 你怎么知道他不尊重老板？

B: _____

练习

一. 根据课文，回答问题

(1) 请介绍一下当今大学生竞聘职位的情况。
(2) 为什么以往的大学生不会面临当今的问题？
(3) 人们对大学生就业观有什么不同的看法？
(4) 学生读了十四、五年书以后去当搓澡工、淘粪工、环卫工，对他们来说，值得吗？

二. 用以下每题所给的词语或句式写出一段话

(1) 招聘 应聘 无疑
(2) 争相 签订 非……不……
(3) 风马牛不相及 迫切 学非所用
(4) 拿……开涮 大材小用 抬高门槛儿
(5) 高不成低不就 碰壁 抢手
(6) ……有之，……有之 上至……，下至…… 总比……强吧

三. 写作练习

谈谈你对大学生竞聘搓澡工、淘粪工、环卫工怎么看。字数: 500–700 字。

四. 讨论

(1) 请通过网络了解中国大学生面临就业问题有哪些方面的原因。
(2) 你认为中国的大学该不该扩招？你认为大学应该是精英化的还是大众化的？大学应该是严进宽出还是宽进严出？
(3) 你认为高学历的人该不该去做低级的工作？作为大学生本人、作为父母、作为大学老师，你怎么看？你认为这是不是人才的浪费？
(4) 有人批评招聘的公司，不需要高学历的工作却让大学生来做，是侮辱大学生，你同意这种观点吗？

五. 辩论

题目: 大学生当搓澡工、淘粪工、环卫工是社会的进步还是退步？
正方: 大学生当搓澡工、淘粪工、环卫工是社会的进步
反方: 大学生当搓澡工、淘粪工、环卫工是社会的退步
辩论的内容可以考虑以下方面:

(1) 社会分工有没有高低贵贱之分？是不是只要是凭自己的劳动能力养活自己就对？
(2) 放下身段、生存第一是否是大学生就业观成熟的表现？
(3) 现在的大学生跟二十年以前的大学生比较，素质一样吗？
(4) 大学生应该为社会提供知识还是体力？
(5) 大学生热衷在城市当搓澡工、淘粪工、环卫工，但是在贫困山区，教师极度缺乏，却没有人愿意去干。个人价值观与社会需求之间是否存在距离？

第三单元

是与非

第5课　爱心恐惧症

Figure 5.1 做了好事, 反而被一口咬定
是撞人者
by Mingming Cheung (2020)

© Mingming Cheung.

Figure 5.2 他撞了我
by Mingming Cheung (2020)

© Mingming Cheung.

Figure 5.3 看到老人摔倒, 是扶还是不扶
by Mingming Cheung (2020)

© Mingming Cheung.

Figure 5.4 赔偿
by Mingming Cheung (2020)

© Mingming Cheung.

　　2006年11月20日，南京水西门广场公共汽车站，两辆公共汽车前后相继进站。等车的老太太徐寿兰从车站跑向后面一辆车，在经过前一辆车后门时不知什么原因跌倒，当时第一个从第一辆车后门下来的彭宇扶起了老太太，和她一起等待家人到来，并和她一起去了医院。徐寿兰跌成了胫骨骨折，治疗花费了数万元。2007年1月12日，徐寿兰向法院起诉彭宇，认定彭宇撞倒了自己，要求他承担医疗费、残疾赔偿金和精神损害。在庭讯中，彭宇否认自己曾与徐寿兰相撞，他说："我下车时是与人相撞了，但不是与原告相撞"，并说自己扶起徐寿兰"是为了做点好事"。

　　在诉讼期间，彭宇打电话给一个网站，说自己做了好事，反而被徐寿兰一口咬定是撞人者，徐寿兰是诬告他，希望媒体关注此案。很多媒体抓住这个事件的道德敏感性，对诉讼过程进行深度报道，于是彭宇案成了全国关注的焦点。经过诉讼，南京地方法院于2007年9月3日作出一审判决，认为"从常理分析，彭宇与原告相撞的可能性较大"，并判决彭宇赔偿徐寿兰4.5万余元。徐寿兰和彭宇都对一审判决提出上诉，但是在二审开庭之前达成和解，彭宇赔偿徐寿兰1万元，双方约定不在媒体上披露和案件有关的信息。

　　彭宇案的判决引起了全国大讨论。看到老人摔倒，扶还是不扶？中国人素以见义勇为、助人为乐为美德，这个问题原本是不需要考虑就可以做出肯定回答的。可是自从彭宇案之后，很多人在回答这个问题时就不那么痛快了；有的人甚至回答说不会去扶。就"扶还是不扶"这个问题，一个网站曾在2011年做过一个调查。近13万名网友参加了调查，其中62.54%的网友选择了"绝对不会，怕惹麻烦"；33.45%的网友认为应该先理性判断，再作决定；仅有4.01%的网友选择应该扶老人，同意"这是起码的公德"。

　　彭宇案发生之后，帮助别人反而惹上官司的事日益增多，人们更不敢轻易向需要帮助的人伸出援助之手。有人把这种现象叫做"爱心恐惧症"。出现在各地的这类"爱心恐惧症"的报道接连不断，最终都指向一个问题：在信任缺失的当今社会，我们还要不要助人为乐、见危施救？关于"爱心恐惧症"的讨论成了舆论关注的热点。

　　一位学者说，在别人需要你帮助的情况下，你不伸出援助之手，在法律上不会惹麻烦，对自己不失为一种万全之策；但如果那位你本来可以救助的人由于没有得到及时救助而延误了治疗的最佳时机，造成不可挽回的损伤甚至死亡，你良心上过得去吗？

　　不少人认为，没有法律作保障，提高社会道德感不过是空谈罢了。有不少人说，施救者应当在救人时提高自我保护意识，在施

救之前最好能找来路人作证或者自行取证。还有人说，如果不能
亲自救助，至少应该拨打报警电话让警察来处理，或者拨打急救
电话，让专业救护人员来施救。

　　总的来说，大部分参加讨论的人都认为整个社会应该倡导在力所
能及的范围内，合理地救助身陷危难的人。不过，对于如何治好爱
心恐惧症，大家都拿不出好的主张来。

　　然而彭宇案到这里并没有尘埃落定。随着时间的推移，彭宇
案又发生了让人目瞪口呆的反转。事件发生六年后，《瞭望新闻
周刊》征得彭、徐双方的同意，发表了对彭宇案的澄清报道。
《瞭望》的记者了解到，在二审和解之前，南京中级法院找到的
报警记录显示"彭宇和徐寿兰均表示与对方发生了碰撞。"（《瞭
望新闻周刊》2012年1月16日：《南京官方称彭宇承认与当事人发
生碰撞　赔偿1万》）　由于双方在和解后的六年中都对媒体三缄
其口，人们一直以为彭宇是助人为乐反被诬告，并由此诊断出中
国社会的爱心恐惧症。原来这六年之中被人们当作中国道德滑
坡的彭宇案其实是假想的，但是假想的彭宇案引爆的爱心恐惧症
却是真的。这前前后后的真真假假和曲曲折折，确实是让人感慨
万千。

第5课　愛心恐懼症

　　2006年11月20日，南京水西門廣場公共汽車站，兩輛公共汽車前
後相繼進站。等車的老太太徐壽蘭從車站跑向后面一輛車，在經
過前一輛車后門時不知什麼原因跌倒，當時第一個從第一輛車后
門下來的彭宇扶起了老太太，和她一起等待家人到來，並和她一
起去了醫院。徐壽蘭跌成了脛骨骨折，治療花費了數萬元。2007
年1月12日，徐壽蘭向法院起訴彭宇，認定彭宇撞倒了自己，要求
他承擔醫療費、殘疾賠償金和精神損害。在庭訊中，彭宇否認自
己曾與徐壽蘭相撞，他說："我下車時是與人相撞了，但不是與原
告相撞"。並說自己扶起徐壽蘭"是為了做點好事"。

　　在訴訟期間，彭宇打電話給一個網站，說自己做了好事，反而
被徐壽蘭一口咬定是撞人者，徐壽蘭是誣告他，希望媒體關注此
案。很多媒體抓住這個事件的道德敏感性，對訴訟過程進行深
度報道，於是彭宇案成了全國關注的焦點。經過訴訟，南京地方
法院於2007年9月3日作出一審判決，認為　"從常理分析，彭宇與原
告相撞的可能性較大"，並判決彭宇賠償徐壽蘭4.5萬余元。徐壽
蘭和彭宇都對一審判決提出上訴，但是在二審開庭之前達成和
解，彭宇賠償徐壽蘭1萬元，雙方約定不在媒體上披露和案件有關
的信息。

　　彭宇案的判決引起了全國大討論。看到老人摔倒，扶還是不扶？中國人素以見義勇為、助人為樂為美德，這個問題原本是不需要考慮就可以做出肯定回答的。可是自從彭宇案之後，很多人在回答這個問題時就不那麼痛快了；有的人甚至回答說不會去扶。就"扶還是不扶"這個問題，一個網站曾在2011年做過一個調查。近13萬名網友參加了調查，其中62.54%的網友選擇了"絕對不會，怕惹麻煩"；33.45%的網友認為應該先理性判斷，再作決定；僅有4.01%的網友選擇應該扶老人，同意"這是起碼的公德"。

　　彭宇案發生之后，幫助別人反而惹上官司的事日益增多，人們更不敢輕易向需要幫助的人伸出援助之手。有人把這種現象叫做"愛心恐懼症"。出現在各地的這類"愛心恐懼症"的報道接連不斷，最終都指向一個問題：在信任缺失的當今社會，我們還要不要助人為樂、見危施救？關於"愛心恐懼症"的討論成了輿論關注的熱點。

　　一位學者說，在別人需要你幫助的情況下，你不伸出援助之手，在法律上不會惹麻煩，對自己不失為一種萬全之策；但如果那位你本來可以救助的人由於沒有得到及時救助而延誤了治療的最佳時機，造成不可挽回的損傷甚至死亡，你良心上過得去嗎？

　　不少人認為，沒有法律作保障，提高社會道德感不過是空談罷了。有不少人，說施救者應當在救人時提高自我保護意識，在施救之前最好能找來路人作証或者自行取証。還有人說，如果不能親自救助，至少應該撥打報警電話讓警察來處理，或者撥打急救電話，讓專業救護人員來施救。

　　總的來說，大部分參加討論的人都認為整個社會應該倡導在力所能及的范圍內，合理地救助身陷危難的人。不過，對於如何治好愛心恐懼症，大家都拿不出好的主張來。

　　然而彭宇案到這裡並沒有塵埃落定。隨著時間的推移，彭宇案又發生了讓人目瞪口呆的反轉。事件發生六年后，《瞭望新聞周刊》征得彭、徐雙方的同意，發表了對彭宇案的澄清報道。《瞭望》的記者了解到，在二審和解之前，南京中級法院找到的報警記錄顯示"彭宇和徐壽蘭均表示與對方發生了碰撞。"（《瞭望新聞周刊》2012年1月16日：《南京官方稱彭宇承認與當事人發生碰撞 賠償1萬》）由於雙方在和解后的六年中都對媒體三緘其口，人們一直以為彭宇是助人為樂反被誣告，並由此診斷出中國社會的愛心恐懼症。原來這六年之中被人們當作中國道德滑坡的彭宇案其實是假想的，但是假想的彭宇案引爆的愛心恐懼症卻是真的。這前前后后的真真假假和曲曲折折，確實是讓人感慨萬千。

新词语

爱心	愛心	àixīn	loving heart; compassion 一颗~/充满~
恐惧	恐懼	kǒngjù	fear; to be afraid of 带来~/对战争的~/我们最~的事发生了/~未知
症	症	zhèng	disease; 病 恐高~/老年痴呆~
跌倒	跌倒	diēdǎo	to fall down ~在地/在路上~了
扶	扶	fú	to help someone up; to support with one's hand 把他~起来/~着墙站起来
胫骨	腔骨	jìnggǔ	shin ~断裂
骨折	骨折	gǔzhé	to fracture; fracture 他的手~了/X光片证实他没有~
起诉	起訴	qǐsù	to sue; to prosecute 妻子~丈夫, 要求离婚/他因杀人罪受到~
认定	認定	rèndìng	to believe firmly; to set one's mind on something or someone 老师~那篇作文是佳作/他~人是善良的/我们要~前进的目标/她终于~他为终身伴侣
承担	承擔	chéngdān	to bear; to undertake ~责任/~一项重要任务
残疾	殘疾	cánjí	physical disability; physically handicapped 身体~/~人
赔偿	賠償	péicháng	to compensate; compensation ~损失/经济~
庭讯	庭訊	tíngxùn	court hearing 那次~长达八小时
相撞	相撞	xiāngzhuàng	to collide; collision 她开的小汽车和一辆从反方向来的卡车~了/两列火车~事故 (shìgù accident)
原告	原告	yuángào	plaintiff ~无话可辩
诬告	誣告	wūgào	to accuse falsely; false accusation 受到~/不可随便~他人/这恐怕是~/对他人进行~
关注	關注	guānzhù	to pay close attention to; deep concern 整个城市都~着这次的足球赛/这是引人~的问题
诉讼	訴訟	sùsòng	lawsuit; 诉: 控告; to charge; 讼: 打官司; to sue 他考虑提起~/法官驳回 (bóhuí to turn down) 了~
一审	一審	yìshěn	trial of first instance ~指法院对案件的最初一级审判
二审	二審	èrshěn	trial of second instance (appeal) ~又称上诉审程序
判决	判決	pànjué	verdict; to be decided by a court 听法官宣布~/这个案子尚未~
上诉	上訴	shàngsù	appeal; to appeal ~失败/无权~
和解	和解	héjiě	legal settlement; to settle; 双方达成妥协~的内容/此案已在庭外~
披露	披露	pīlù	to lay bare ~实情/不要向别人~个人资料
见义勇为	見義勇為	jiàn yì yǒng wéi	to do what is morally right; 见到应该做的事, 勇敢地去做 他~, 牺牲了生命/~的英雄
助人为乐	助人為樂	zhù rén wéi lè	to take pleasure in helping others 他们~, 做了很多好事/~的行为
惹	惹	rě	to invite or ask for; to provoke ~祸 (huò disaster)/~人注目/~人生气/别~人讨厌

起码	起碼	qǐmǎ	minimum; at least 言行一致是做人~的准则/礼貌是对人~的尊重/她~四十岁了/我们做作业~要半天
公德	公德	gōngdé	public morality 社会~/没有~
官司	官司	guānsī	lawsuit; "诉讼"俗称"官司" 惹上~/打赢~/输了~
现象	現象	xiànxiàng	phenomenon 表面~/自然~
万全之策	萬全之策	wàn quán zhī cè	foolproof strategy; 万分周到的办法 想出一个~/找出~
及时	及時	jíshí	on time; right away 医生~救了他一命/我尽全力~完成了工作
延误	延誤	yánwù	delay; to incur loss through delay 航班~/~治疗
不可挽回	不可挽回	bù kě wǎnhuí	irreparable 海洋污染造成~的鱼类损失/~的后果
良心	良心	liángxīn	conscience 没有~/~发现/~不安
过得去	過得去	guòdéqù	able to get by; passable 他面子上~/我们生活还~/他日语还~/他不是个好运动员，但还~
作证	作证	zuòzhèng	to testify 去法庭~/我为你~
自行	自行	zìxíng	by oneself ~处理/~解决
取证	取證	qǔzhèng	to collect evidence 多方~/如何~
报警	報警	bàojǐng	to report an emergency to the police ~求助/打电话~
倡导	倡導	chàngdǎo	to advocate ~和平/~自由
尘埃落定	塵埃落定	chén āi luò dìng	to settle; to end; literally, the dust settles; 尘埃: 灰尘, 尘土; 落: 掉下来; 定: 不动, 不变; 比喻经过变化, 终于有了确定的结果 比赛名次已经~/战争何时~
目瞪口呆	目瞪口呆	mù dèng kǒu dāi	dumbstruck; 也可以说"瞠目结舌" (chēng mù jié shé 瞠着眼睛说不出话来, 形容吃惊的样子) 吓得~/一时~, 不知如何反应
反转	反轉	fǎnzhuǎn	reversal 房价出现了~/股票市场一周前急速~
瞭望	瞭望	liàowàng	to look out over; lookout ~远方/~塔
澄清	澄清	chéngqīng	to clarify ~误会/~事实
记录	記錄	jìlù	record; to record 采访~/~生活经历/~社会变迁
三缄其口	三緘其口	sān jiān qí kǒu	to refuse to speak as if one's mouth were sealed; 形容说话很谨慎; 缄: to seal 对于不了解的事, 我们最好~/一提起家事, 他就~
诊断	診斷	zhěnduàn	to diagnose; diagnosis 他请医生~他的病/医生作出~
滑坡	滑坡	huápō	decline; to be on the decline; landslide 经济~/质量~/某些地方的生产在~/经济危机使房地产~/河流两边产生了~现象/我们必须防治~
曲曲折折	曲曲折折	qū qū zhé zhé	ups and downs; winding 经历了许多~/~的道路
感慨万千	感慨萬千	gǎn kǎi wàn qiān	to be filled with nostalgic feelings; 因外界事物变化很大而引起许多感想 看到家乡的变化, 他~/三十年后再次相遇, 他们~

重点词语和句式

1 一口咬定 (to state with absolute certainty; to cling to one's view; to state categorically; 一口咬住不放, 比喻不顾事实或在没有证据的情况下坚持一个说法。)

    (1) 徐寿兰一口咬定 (彭宇) 是撞人者。
    (Xu Shou-lan stated with absolute certainty that Peng Yu was the person who had bumped into her.)

    (2) 她一口咬定钱是那个孩子偷走的。
    (She clung to the idea that that child had stolen her money.)

    (3) 自从警察审问我以后, 以前经常见面的那个商店老板现在一口咬定不认识我。
    (Ever since the police interrogated me, the shopkeeper whom I used to see often has stated categorically that he doesn't know me.)

翻译:

    (1) He is accused of robbing a bank, but his older brother clings to the idea that he is innocent.

    ———————————————————————

    (2) Before Columbus made his voyages, many people believed with absolute certainty that the Earth was flat.

    ———————————————————————

2 素以……为…… (to have always regarded something as; 向来以……是……)

    (1) 中国人素以见义勇为、助人为乐为美德。
    (The Chinese have always regarded acting bravely for a just cause and taking pleasure in helping others as virtues.)

    (2) 雇佣者素以工作申请截止日期前的邮戳 (yóuchuō postmark) 为凭, 判断应聘者的申请是否有效。
    (Employers have always considered job applications timely as long as they have been postmarked by the deadline.)

    (3) 他喜爱欧洲文化, 素以曾在欧洲留学为荣。
    (He loves European culture. He has always been proud of having studied in Europe.)

翻译:

    (1) 中国人素以历史、文化悠久为傲。

    ———————————————————————

    (2) 他很注意养生, 饮食素以清淡为主。

    ———————————————————————

3 日益增多 (an increasing number; more and more; 一天比一天多)

    (1) 帮助人反而惹上官司的事日益增多。
    (There had been an increasing number of cases where Good Samaritans ended up being sued by the very people they had tried to help.)

(2) 近几年来加拿大的移民日益增多。
(In recent years, an increasing number of immigrants have arrived in Canada.)

(3) 在中国, 买车的人日益增多。
(In China, more and more people are buying cars.)

翻译:

(1) There are an increasing number of educational exchanges between China and the U.S.

_____

(2) In the winter, more and more people are catching the flu.

_____

4 接连不断 (over and over again; to go on continually; endless succession; 一个接着
   一个; 不间断)

(1) 出现在各地的这类"爱心恐惧症"的报道接连不断。
(Cases of bystanders hesitating to help people out of fear of being sued turned up over and over again in different places.)

(2) 不知为什么, 今天电话接连不断。
(Nobody knows why there has been a continual stream of phone calls today.)

(3) 接连不断的晚宴把我们累坏了。
(The endless succession of dinner parties wore us out.)

翻译:

(1) Recently, there have been continual snowstorms. Many residents' homes have been destroyed.

_____

(2) This restaurant is very popular. It always has a steady stream of customers.

_____

5 不失为 (might in fact; nevertheless; indeed; "不"、"失"都是否定词, 否定的否定, 就
   是肯定; 还算得上是)

(1) 一位学者说, 在别人需要你帮助的情况下, 你不伸出援助之手, 在法律上可能
    不会惹麻烦, 对自己不失为一种万全之策。
(A scholar said that if someone needed your assistance and you did not extend a helping hand, you would probably not be violating the law and might in fact save yourself a great deal of trouble.)

(2) 他有缺点, 但是他不失为好人。
(He has his weaknesses, but he is nevertheless a good man.)

(3) 那家购物中心商店众多, 不失为购物者的天堂。
(That shopping mall has a huge number of stores; it is indeed a shoppers' paradise.)

翻译:

    (1) Although this house is shabby, it could nevertheless serve as a valuable investment.

    ———————————————————————————————————

    (2) Although he didn't win the gold medal this time, he is nevertheless an excellent athlete.

    ———————————————————————————————————

6   空谈 (empty talk; to indulge in empty talk; 纸上谈兵, 发表空论, 没有实践)

    (1) 不少人士认为, 没有法律作保障, 提高社会道德感不过是空谈罢了。
    (Many people think that, without legal protection, calls to raise the standard of public morality are just empty talk.)

    (2) 想法再好可是没有具体措施也是空谈。
    (No matter how good the ideas are, without concrete measures, they are all empty talk.)

    (3) 我不喜欢空谈, 喜欢做实事。
    (I don't like to engage in empty talk; I am a man of action.)

翻译:

    (1) Enough of your empty talk! I don't want to hear it anymore.

    ———————————————————————————————————

    (2) Concrete action is better than empty talk.

    ———————————————————————————————————

7   力所能及 (within one's power or ability; 力: 体力, 能力; 及: 达到; 力量能够达到的范围)

    (1) 大部分参加讨论的人都认为整个社会应该倡导在力所能及的范围内, 合理地救助身陷危难的人。
    (Most people who joined the discussion believed that society as a whole should encourage citizens to take all reasonable measures within their powers to rescue those in danger.)

    (2) 他很热心, 总是力所能及地帮助别人。
    (He is very kindhearted; he always does whatever is within his power to help others.)

    (3) 我不会做生意, 开公司非我力所能及。
    (I don't know how to do business. Starting a company is not within my ability.)

翻译:

    (1) I have done everything within my power. Sorry, I can't help you more.

    ———————————————————————————————————

    (2) After he retired, he did all he could to help the homeless.

    ———————————————————————————————————

练习

一．根据课文，回答问题

(1)　请介绍一下彭宇案。
(2)　彭宇和徐寿兰谁利用大众媒体为自己辩解？为什么？
(3)　请从徐寿兰的角度讲述彭宇案中发生的事。
(4)　彭宇案判决以后网上调查情况如何？引起什么样的讨论？
(5)　六年以后，《瞭望新闻周刊》怎么报道彭宇案？

二．用以下每题所给的词语或句式写出一段话

(1)　承担　赔偿　关注
(2)　起诉　日益增多　一口咬定
(3)　搀扶　承担　不失为
(4)　延误　感慨万千　三缄其口
(5)　空谈　力所能及　接连不断

三．至少用三个新词语回答以下每个问题，请在新词语下面划出一道线

(1)　你看见一个老人摔倒后，你把老人扶了起来。记者采访你时，问你这样做有没有顾虑。你怎么回答？
(2)　你看见一个老人摔倒后，你只是给警察打电话，并没有把老人扶起来。记者采访你时，问你为什么这样做。你怎么回答？
(3)　某地政府决定设立助人为乐基金。你是政府的官员，记者采访你，问你为什么政府要这样做。你怎么回答？

四．讨论

(1)　通过网络详细了解南京彭宇案的情节。(彭宇的说法，徐寿兰的说法，特别是法官的说法都是什么？六年后真相大白是什么意思？)
(2)　人们患"爱心恐惧症"的原因有哪些，彭宇案是唯一的原因吗？
(3)　在你的国家有没有跟彭宇案类似的新闻？请介绍给大家。
(4)　2017年10月中国"好人法"正式实施，规定"因自愿实施紧急救助行为造成受助人损害的，救助人不承担民事责任"。有了"好人法"，大家是否会积极伸出援手？
(5)　其他国家有"好人法"吗？如何防范被援助者事后反咬一口？见死不救者如何处罚？

五．辩论

题目：老人跌倒该不该搀扶？
正方：老人跌倒应该搀扶
反方：老人跌倒不应该搀扶
请注意"搀扶"的含义："搀扶"字面上是瞬时性动作，但在实际的用法中兼有援助之意，是延续性动作。
辩论的内容可以考虑以下方面：

(1)　是不是法律没有规定，我们就不应该去搀扶摔倒的老人？
(2)　摔倒以后，大多数老人会起诉扶起他们的人吗？
(3)　我们的社会有"信任危机"吗？
(4)　不帮助老人是一种必要的自我保护、可以理解的行为还是一种怕惹麻烦的、自私的行为？
(5)　从道德观点来看，我们应该尊敬老人、帮助老人吗？

第6课　地动山摇中的选择

Figure 6.1 范是第一个到达足球场的人
by Mingming Cheung (2020)

© Mingming Cheung.

Figure 6.2 民意地震
by Mingming Cheung (2020)

© Mingming Cheung.

Figure 6.3 群起而攻之
by Mingming Cheung (2020)

© Mingming Cheung.

Figure 6.4 范美忠赢得了一个绰号"范跑跑"
by Mingming Cheung (2020)

© Mingming Cheung.

2008年5月12日，汶川大地震。在离震中仅三公里的都江堰市光亚中学，时任语文老师的范美忠正在给学生上课。事后范美忠回忆起当时的情形："课桌晃动了一下，学生一愣，有点不知所措。因为此前经历过几次桌子和床晃动的轻微地震，所以我对地震有一些经验，我镇定自若地安抚学生：'不要慌！地震，没事……'话还没完，教学楼猛烈地震动起来，甚至发出哗哗的响声，我瞬间反应过来——大地震！然后猛然向楼梯冲过去，在下楼的时候甚至摔了一跤，这个时候我突然闪过一个念头：'难道中国遭到了核袭击？'然后连滚带爬地以最快速度冲到了教学楼旁边的足球场中央！我发现自己居然是第一个到达足球场的人。"

不幸中的万幸，范美忠所教的学生没有伤亡，光亚中学的师生也都安然无恙。比起震区其他学校惨烈的伤亡，这个事件在汶川大地震中并不引人注目。但是范美忠后来在著名的网站"天涯"上发的帖子使他成为舆论的焦点。在《那一刻地动山摇》中，范美忠自省为什么不组织学生撤离就跑了："其实，那一瞬间屋子晃动得如此厉害，我知道自己只是本能反应而已。……不过，瞬间的本能抉择却可能反映了内在的自我与他人生命孰为重的权衡。……在这种生死抉择的瞬间，只有为了我的女儿我才考虑牺牲自我，其他的人，哪怕是我的母亲，在这种情况下我也不会管的。"

这篇帖子引发了网络和主流媒体上的民意地震，成为汶川大地震中的一个争论焦点。激愤者蜂拥而至，对范美忠群起而攻之，也有少数人捍卫他讲真话的权利。在这场争论中尤其引人注目的是范美忠的知识分子身份，他毕业于北京大学历史系，经常针砭时弊，对中国的教育体制和政治体制都多有批判，他的教学不落俗套，鼓励学生独立思考。但是，就是这样一个本应为人师表的老师，这样一个本应秉持公义的知识分子，却在生死一线的刹那间弃学生于不顾。他事后虽向学生和学校道歉，但仍然坚持自己没有"冒死救学生的义务"。这样的反差，放到舆论漩涡中，被无限倍地放大。范美忠赢得了一个绰号"范跑跑"。

范美忠事件，就像有些发生在中国的其他事件一样，很快就被拿来与西方国家作比较。有人说："范美忠事件如果发生在美国，他铁定会被学校开除，而且这辈子别想当教师了。原因很简单：他的所作所为非常不具有职业道德。"作为一个老师，弃学生的生命不顾而独自逃跑确实有违基本道德准则。受范美忠事件的影响，中国教育部在2008年6月26日公布修改后的《中小学教师职业道德规范》，首次列入"保护学生安全"。

事隔多年，当人们对汶川地震的许多记忆逐渐褪去之后，"范跑跑"这个名字却未被轻易忘记。尘埃落定之后，又有人评论："我们是否想过范美忠为何要逃跑呢？如果你的房子足够坚固，让所有人都觉得那是安全之地，范美忠为何要跑呢？如果你对范美忠等所有老师进行过真正的安全教育，学生的安全教育也同步实施，大家都训练有素，那么范美忠为何要跑呢?"

我们可以把校舍安全和对教师安全教育的缺失放到更大的道德环境里，继续追问下去。在目前的中国，利他行为有时会受骗上当，见义勇为有时会遭到报复，对有的人来说最合理的选择就是自保。范美忠的逃跑到底有多少是出于自保的反应，有多少是出于把自己的生命看得重于他人，恐怕是一个连他自己也难以回答的问题。

第6课　地动山搖中的選擇

2008年5月12日，汶川大地震。在離震中僅三公裡的都江堰市光亞中學，時任語文老師的范美忠正在給學生上課。事后范美忠回憶起當時的情形："課桌晃動了一下，學生一愣，有點不知所措。因為此前經歷過幾次桌子和床晃動的輕微地震，所以我對地震有一些經驗，我鎮定自若地安撫學生：'不要慌！地震，沒事……'話還沒完，教學樓猛烈地震動起來，甚至發出嘩嘩的響聲，我瞬間反應過來——大地震！然后猛然向樓梯衝過去，在下樓的時候甚至摔了一跤，這個時候我突然閃過一個念頭：'難道中國遭到了核襲擊？'然后連滾帶爬地以最快速度衝到了教學樓旁邊的足球場中央！我發現自己居然是第一個到達足球場的人。"

不幸中的萬幸，范美忠所教的學生沒有傷亡，光亞中學的師生也都安然無恙。比起震區其他學校慘烈的傷亡，這個事件在汶川大地震中並不引人注目。但是范美忠后來在著名的網站"天涯"上發的帖子使他成為輿論的焦點。在《那一刻地動山搖》中，範美忠自省為什麼不組織學生撤離就跑了："其實，那一瞬間屋子晃動得如此厲害，我知道自己只是本能反應而已。……不過，瞬間的本能抉擇卻可能反映了內在的自我與他人生命孰為重的權衡。……在這種生死抉擇的瞬間，只有為了我的女兒我才考慮犧牲自我，其他的人，哪怕是我的母親，在這種情況下我也不會管的。"

這篇帖子引發了網絡和主流媒體上的民意地震，成為汶川大地震中的一個爭論焦點。激憤者蜂擁而至，對范美忠群起而攻之，也有少數人捍衛他講真話的權利。在這場爭論中尤其引人注目的是范美忠的知識分子身份：他畢業於北京大學歷史系，經常針砭時弊，對中國的教育體制和政治體制都多有批判，他的教學不落俗套，鼓勵學生獨立思考。但是，就是這樣一個本應為人師表的老師，這樣一個本應秉持公義的知識份子，卻在生死一線的剎那間棄學生於不顧。他事后雖向學生和學校道歉，但仍然堅持自己沒有"冒死救學生的義務"。這樣的反差，放到輿論漩渦中，更是被無限倍地放大。范美忠贏得了一個綽號"范跑跑"。

范美忠事件，就像有些發生在中國的其他事件一樣，很快就被拿來與西方國家作比較。有人說："范美忠事件如果發生在美國，他鐵定會被學校開除，而且這輩子別想當教師了。原因很簡單：他的所作所為非常不具有職業道德。"作為一個老師，棄學生的生命不顧而獨自逃跑確實有違基本道德準則。受范美忠事件的影響，中國教育部在2008年6月26日公布修改后的《中小學教師職業道德規範》，首次列入"保護學生安全"。

事隔多年，當人們對汶川地震的許多記憶逐漸褪去之后，"范跑跑"這個名字卻未被輕易忘記。塵埃落定之后，又有人評論："我們是否想過范美忠為何要逃跑呢？如果你的房子足夠堅固，讓所有人都覺得那是安全之地，范美忠為何要跑呢？如果你對范美忠等所有老師進行過真正的安全教育，學生的安全教育也同步實施，大家都訓練有素，那麼范美忠為何要跑呢？"

我們可以把校舍安全和對教師安全教育的缺失放到更大的道德環境裡，繼續追問下去。在目前的中國，利他行為有時會受騙上當，見義勇為有時會遭到報復，因此對有的人來說最合理的選擇就是自保。范美忠的逃跑到底有多少是出於自保的反應，有多少是出於把自己的生命看得重於他人，恐怕是一個連他自己也難以回答的問題。

新词语

汶川	汶川	Wènchuān	a county in Sichuan Province; 四川省县名
都江堰	都江堰	Dūjiāng Yàn	Dujiang Irrigation System; 在四川省都江堰市城西
晃动	晃動	huàngdòng	to sway 地震使房子来回~/微风中小树轻轻地~着
一愣	一愣	yílèng	to be taken aback 吓得~/不觉~
不知所措	不知所措	bù zhī suǒ cuò	to be at a loss as to what to do; 不知道怎么办才好 事情来得突然，他~/他被骂得~
镇定自若	鎮定自若	zhèn dìng zì ruò	to remain calm; 镇定:不慌乱; 若:跟以往一样 面对敌人，他~/房子失火了，他却~
安抚	安撫	ānfǔ	to calm; 安定抚慰 ~遇难者家属/~他悲伤的心情
猛烈	猛烈	měngliè	violently; violent ~地摇来摇去/~地攻击/~的风暴/~的战争
瞬间	瞬間	shùnjiān	in the blink of an eye; 刹那 ~不见了/~的变化
冲	衝	chōng	to dash; 不顾一切,一直向前 ~过红灯/~下山去
闪	閃	shǎn	to flash 灯光一~/窗外~过一个人影

念头	念頭	niàntóu	idea; thought; 想法 放弃买车的~/动过结婚的~
遭到	遭到	zāodào	to encounter; 碰到 ~拒绝/~惩罚/~批评
核袭击	核襲擊	hé xíjī	nuclear attack 发动~/面临~
连滚带爬	連滾帶爬	lián gǔn dài pá	to flee in fear; literally, to both roll and crawl; 形容因害怕而逃走的样子 警察来了, 小偷~地跑了/海啸来了, 他们~地离开岸边
安然无恙	安然無恙	ān rán wú yàng	safe and sound 我们担心走失的孩子是否~/虽然~, 她还是受了点惊吓
惨烈	慘烈	cǎnliè	severe 竞争~/~的车祸
伤亡	傷亡	shāngwáng	injuries and deaths; casualties ~人数/~巨大
引人注目	引人注目	yǐn rén zhù mù	noticeable; to catch one's eye; 吸引人注意 ~的进步/~的色彩
网站	網站	wǎngzhàn	website ~信息/社交~
天涯	天涯	tiānyá	the end of the world 海角~/走~
帖子	帖子	tiězi	a message posted on the internet 发~/回复~
舆论	輿論	yúlùn	public opinion 公众~不一致/~是反对战争
自省	自省	zìxǐng	to reflect upon one's mistakes; 自我检讨 出了那么大的问题, 你应该好好儿~一下
撤离	撤離	chèlí	to evacuate; 撤退离开 ~危险地带/~城市
本能反应	本能反應	běnnéng fǎnyìng	instinctive reaction 恐惧是对危险的~/抓到坏人以后, 他的~是把坏人交给警察
内在	內在	nèizài	inner ~美/~力量/~矛盾
自我	自我	zìwǒ	self ~介绍/~中心/~限制
孰	孰	shú	which; 哪个 ~轻~重/~优~劣/~先~后
权衡	權衡	quánhéng	the weighing of priorities; to weigh; originally, scale; 权: 锤 (chuí the counterweight of a steelyard balance); 衡: 秤 (chèng steelyard balance) 政策~/利弊~/~轻重/~得失
引发	引發	yǐnfā	to lead to; to trigger; 引起 ~许多问题/~改革
网络	網絡	wǎngluò	internet; network ~电视台/无线~
主流	主流	zhǔliú	mainstream ~报刊/非~文化
民意	民意	mínyì	the will and desire of the people; public opinion; 民众的意愿 了解~/~调查 (public opinion poll)
激愤	激憤	jīfèn	indignant; enraged; indignation; 激动愤怒 ~的演说/心情~/引起一片~
蜂拥而至	蜂擁而至	fēng yōng ér zhì	to arrive in great numbers like a swarm of bees; 像一窝蜂似地拥来 观者~/~的难民
群起而攻之	群起而攻之	qún qǐ ér gōng zhī	to join in attacking someone or something 他品德低劣, 难怪大家~/有些人看到与主流观点不同的意见, 马上~
捍卫	捍衛	hànwèi	to defend ~家园/~自由
知识分子	知識分子	zhīshí fènzǐ	intellectual 高级~/~家庭

针砭时弊	針砭時弊	zhēn biān shí bì	to diagnose social ills; 针砭:古代的一种针刺疗法,现在已经失传; 时弊:现时的缺点 他的文章/他借古讽今,~
不落俗套	不落俗套	bú luò sú tào	not to conform to conventions; 不用陈旧的格式 这首诗清新、~/他艺术风格~,独特自然
为人师表	為人師表	wéi rén shī biǎo	to be worthy of being called a teacher; to be a paragon of virtue and learning; 师表:榜样; model; example 教师的工作就是~/在~方面, 李老师很成功
秉持	秉持	bǐngchí	to uphold; 主持; 秉:拿着; 持:拿着; 握住 ~原则/~公正之心
公义	公義	gōngyì	justice 主持~/伸张~
生死一线	生死一線	shēng sǐ yí xiàn	the thin line between life and death 在~之间 /身处~间
冒死	冒死	màosǐ	to brave death ~救人/~抗敌
反差	反差	fǎnchā	contrast 高~/形成强烈~
漩涡	漩渦	xuánwō	swirl 水流形成的螺旋形水涡,比喻某种不能使人解脱的境地 河水打着~/他陷入了爱情的~
无限	無限	wúxiàn	infinite 前途~光明/有~的潜力
倍	倍	bèi	to double; times (as in multiplication) 他的工资增长了两~/弟弟比他高大一~/这事比想象困难十~/他比我聪明一万~
绰号	綽號	chuòhào	nickname; 外号 取~/起~
铁定	鐵定	tiědìng	definitely ~成功/~有希望/~会被气死
开除	開除	kāichú	to expel; to dismiss 遭到学校~/被单位~了
公布	公佈	gōngbù	to promulgate; to announce ~法令/~政策/~计划/~罪状
修改	修改	xiūgǎi	to amend; to revise ~合同/~作品
规范	規範	guīfàn	code; 规定 伦理~/学生行为~
事隔多年	事隔多年	shì gé duō nián	after many years ~,那场车祸还在我的脑海中/没想到~你还记得那件事
褪去	褪去	tuìqù	to fade 雾慢慢/西边的晚霞渐渐~
同步	同步	tóngbù	to synchronize; at the same pace 电影的画面和声音不~/农业改革需要与工业改革~进行
实施	實施	shíshī	to implement ~计划/~政策/~规则
训练有素	訓練有素	xùnliàn yǒu sù	well-trained 我们的军队~/我校篮球校队~
校舍	校舍	xiàoshè	school building 修建~/~陈旧
追问	追問	zhuīwèn	to press by asking over and again; 追究事情的原因 只要你认错, 我们就不再~/再~下去, 他就要生气了
受骗	受騙	shòupiàn	to be cheated 花言巧语往往使人~/他发觉~, 非常气愤
上当	上當	shàngdàng	to be fooled; 受骗吃亏 在夜市小摊买东西, 容易~/他很聪明, 绝不会~
自保	自保	zìbǎo	self-protection; to protect oneself 只求~/安于~/难以~/~性命

重点词语和句式

1　时任 (at the time someone was; 时: 当时; 任: 担任)

   (1)　在离震中仅三公里的都江堰市光亚中学, 时任语文老师的范美忠正在给学生上课。
     (Guangya Middle School in the city of Dujiang Yan was only three kilometers from the epicenter. Fan Meizhong, the school's Chinese teacher at the time, was teaching his students.)

   (2)　2015年国民党时任主席马英九与中共中央总书记习近平在新加坡会晤。
     (In 2015, Ma Yingjiu, the KMT Chairman at the time, met with the CCP Secretary General, Xi Jinping, in Singapore.)

   (3)　他在2010年开始为这家建筑公司工作, 时任工程师。
     (He started working for this architectural firm in 2010. At the time, he worked as an engineer.)

用"时任"完成对话:

   (1)　A: 1970年加拿大与中国建交时, 加拿大总理是谁?

     B: _____

   (2)　A: 2014年在俄国举办冬季奥林匹克运动会, 当时俄国总统是谁?

     B: _____

2　不幸中的万幸 (miraculously; to my amazing good fortune; literally, good fortune in the midst of all misfortune; 许多不幸中的幸运)

   (1)　不幸中的万幸, 范美忠所教的学生没有伤亡, 光亚中学的师生也都安然无恙。
     (Miraculously, none of Fan Meizhong's students were injured or killed. All of the teachers and students at Guangya Middle School were safe and sound.)

   (2)　不幸中的万幸, 车祸中没有人受伤。
     (Miraculously, no one was injured in the car accident.)

   (3)　一个醉汉把玻璃瓶从十楼扔到街上, 没有砸 (zá to smash) 到我头上, 真是不幸中的万幸。
     (A drunken man threw a glass bottle from the tenth floor down to the street below. To my amazing good fortune, the bottle missed my head.)

用"不幸中的万幸"完成句子:

   (1)　大火中, 他失去了一切, _____

   (2)　连日大风雪, 家中无电无水, _____

3　A 与 B 孰为重 (which is more important, A or B?)

   (1)　……不过, 瞬间的本能抉择却可能反映了内在的自我与他人生命孰为重的权衡。
     (. . . But perhaps a person's first, instinctive choice revealed the weight of his priorities. Which was more important, his life or the lives of others?)

    (2) 在你心中爱情与金钱孰为重?
       (In your mind, which is more important, love or money?)

    (3) 对一个男人来说, 家庭与事业孰为重?
       (For a man, which is more important, his family or his career?)

翻译:

    (1) 面对危难, 自我与集体孰为重?

    _____

    (2) 当今社会德与才孰为重?

    _____

4   弃……不顾 (to leave someone in the lurch)

    (1) 就是这样一个为人师表的老师, 在生死一线的刹那间弃学生于不顾。
       (He was a model teacher, but in a moment of life and death, he left his students in the lurch.)

    (2) 狠心的儿子弃生病的老父亲不顾。
       (The cruel-hearted son left his sick old father in the lurch.)

    (3) 两人同去游泳, 一人溺水了, 另一人弃同伴不顾。
       (Two people went swimming together. When one began to drown, the other left him in the lurch.)

用"弃……不顾"完成对话:

    (1) 那个孤儿是怎么来到孤儿院的?

    _____

    (2) 他病情严重, 你留下照顾他吧, 我管不了了。

    _____

5   不具有 (to lack); 具有 (to have)

    (1) 他的所作所为非常不具有职业道德。
       (His behavior lacked all professionalism.)

    (2) 你不具有教书经验, 我们需要的是资深教师。
       (You lack any teaching experience. What we need is a highly experienced teacher.)

    (3) 他们都在加拿大出生, 都具有加拿大国籍。
       (They were all born in Canada and have Canadian citizenship.)

翻译:

    (1) What would happen if we lacked hope?

    _____

(2) I have confidence in myself. I know that I will be all right in life.

---

6 有违……准则 (to violate a principle or rule; to be against the law; 违: 违背; 不遵守)

(1) 作为一个老师, 弃学生的生命于不顾而独自逃跑确实有违基本道德准则。
(As a teacher, he violated a basic moral principle. He abandoned his students and fled by himself.)

(2) 闯红灯有违交通准则。
(Running a red light is against the law.)

(3) 那个运动员使用药物提高成绩, 有违世界反禁药组织准则。
(That athlete used drugs to enhance his performance. He violated the rules of the World Anti-Doping Agency.)

用 "有违……准则" 完成句子:

(1) 无医生执照行医有违 _____

(2) 乘客携带危险品上飞机有违 _____

练习

一. 根据课文, 回答问题

(1) 范美忠怎么回忆汶川大地震的情形?
(2) 范美忠的帖子写了什么? 为什么造成争论?
(3) 多年以后, 有人重新评论范美忠的逃跑吗? 如何评论的?
(4) 你所在的国家有没有规定突然发生灾难时老师的责任? 有没有类似范美忠事件的争议和讨论? 调查后给大家介绍。

二. 用以下每题所给的词语或句式写出一段话

(1) 晃动 安抚 连滚带爬
(2) 不幸中的万幸 本能反应 蜂拥而至
(3) 不落俗套 为人师表 绰号
(4) 不具有 事隔多年 追问
(5) 时任 弃……不顾 镇定自若

三. 写作练习

题目: 我看 "范美忠" 事件。 字数: 500–700 字。

四. 讨论

(1) 请通过网络了解汶川地震几年以后范美忠的情况, 他被学校解雇了吗? 他向公众道歉了吗? 他的想法有所改变吗?
(2) 范美忠可不可以跑? 为什么? 范美忠应不应该跑? 为什么? 可以跑和应该跑之间有什么区别?

(3) 支持范美忠的人和反对范美忠的人有哪些分歧？请列举。
(4) 一个国家的道德环境与人在紧急时刻选择自保有关联吗？

五. 辩论

题目: 你对范美忠的言行支持还是反对？
正方: 我支持范美忠的言行
反方: 我反对范美忠的言行
辩论内容可以考虑以下方面:

(1) 范美忠在网上说的话对不对？有没有道理？
(2) 他有没有说真话的权利？网友给他起绰号、讽刺他, 对不对？
(3) 老师的责任到底是什么？在危急情况下, 老师应该怎么做？说一个老师够资格或者不够资格的根据是什么？
(4) 为什么只有很少人赞成范美忠的言行？以集体为本和以个人为本哪个对？
(5) 你对"为人师表"怎么看？

第四单元

中与西

第7课 洋节在中国

Figure 7.1 商家的圣诞节
by Mingming Cheung (2020)

© Mingming Cheung.

Figure 7.2 万圣节
by Mingming Cheung (2020)

© Mingming Cheung.

Figure 7.3 不知丘比特是谁
by Mingming Cheung (2020)

© Mingming Cheung.

Figure 7.4 耶稣是谁
by Mingming Cheung (2020)

© Mingming Cheung.

　　洋节在中国越来越受到年轻人的青睐。他们中不少人对西方的圣诞节、万圣节、情人节、愚人节等如数家珍，可要是说起中国传统节日的具体日子，能答全的却寥寥无几。网络上、媒体上关于"洋节"、"土节"的辩论随处可见。最引人注目的莫过于2006年12月10名中国名校的博士联名发出的抵制圣诞节、抵御西方文化扩张的倡议书，一时间掀起了一阵"圣诞节过还是不过"的争议。往后每年圣诞来临之际，常有土洋交锋。

　　我跟朋友聊到洋节在中国流行的原因时，朋友的说法颇有代表性。他说，在生活节奏日益紧张的今天，借着洋节的名，约几个朋友聚聚，天南海北侃侃，释放压力，加深友情，交流信息，换来一个好心情，何乐而不为？不知道那些洋节的来历又有何妨？对老百姓来说，甭管是洋节、土节，只要让人过得开心就行。另外，我发现，国人过洋节的那份狂热，还应该归功于商家的推波助澜。最典型的要数圣诞节了，商家通过渲染节日气氛，推出一系列圣诞优惠购物活动，激起消费欲望，然后大赚一笔。最后，还有一个原因恐怕跟文化优势有关。不要说我们的土节，就是佛教、伊斯兰教的节日也同样敌不过基督教背景的圣诞节。这倒不是说中国人对基督教更认同，而是圣诞节让人联想到的是欧美发达国家的生活方式，在普通老百姓眼里代表的是一种富裕、悠闲的生活方式，作为一个老百姓，谁不希望自己能跟富裕的文明靠近一点呢？

　　一些学者认为，不同的地理、文化、历史、风俗习惯造就了不同国家的节日，但这并不妨碍人们在节日上互通有无。节日作为文化的一部分，应该是兼容并蓄的。举个例子来说，我们的父母为我们辛苦操劳，养育之恩无以回报，因而在"父亲节"、"母亲节"特别为父母做一件事，表达一份心意，应该是一件很值得肯定的事，过这样的洋节不是更能弘扬中华民族尊老敬老的传统美德吗？其他一些节日，比如圣诞节，如果能让人们在这些节日相互祝福、与亲朋好友共度一段闲暇时光，也是无可厚非的。还有诸如愚人节、万圣节之类单纯用来消遣和娱乐的洋节，给大家开玩笑的借口、穿得奇形怪状的机会，给一成不变的生活增加点亮色，何乐而不为？在某些人眼里，过洋节就是崇洋媚外的标志。实际上，在这样一个全球化的时代，非议过洋节，或者想把某种文化拒之门外，是不切实际的，也是没有必要的；更好的办法是借助逐渐强大的国力，将自己的传统文化推向世界，在与别国文化的交流和碰撞中，寻求传统文化的立足点，并以此丰富世界文化。

　　也有人指出，洋节的兴起与我们目前思想的开放、追求生活方式的西化、对西方文化的盲从是分不开的。不错，洋节在某种程度上是我们了解外国风情、了解世界各族文化的窗口。可洋节毕竟是洋人的节日，中国人过洋节，往往过的是洋节的"皮"，根本不知道"瓤"是什么。2月14日给女朋友送999朵玫瑰，却不知丘比特是谁；圣诞之夜又蹦又跳地去抢礼物，可连耶稣的来历都还没搞清，这样的人大有人在。说到圣诞节，那是个宗教节日，要是你一不看《圣经》，二不做礼拜，过哪门子圣诞呀！从深层来讲，过洋节其实是弱势民族在追求现代化过程中对强势民族的一种仿效行为。我们中国有自己的民族文化，而且绝不是一种劣等文化。对那些洋节，我们应该说"不"。

还有一位学者在接受记者采访时表示，我们不应该简单地拒绝"洋节"，因为外来节日充实了我们的文化生活；当然也决不能丢弃自己的节日，因为传统节日是民族文化的精髓，如果毁弃，是对历史的不负责任。同时，传统节日也是传承文化最好的载体。在全球化的时代，世界正变得越来越雷同，这时候，民族文化往往是最值得珍惜的资源。因此，我们要重视和保护我们的传统，并把它发扬光大。

第7課 洋節在中國

洋節在中國越來越受到年輕人的青睞。他們中不少人對西方的聖誕節、萬聖節、情人節、愚人節等如數家珍，可要是說起中國傳統節日的具體日子，能答全的卻寥寥無幾。網絡上、媒體上關於"洋節"、"土節"的辯論隨處可見。最引人注目的莫過於2006年12月10名中國名校的博士聯名發出的抵制聖誕節、抵御西方文化擴張的倡議書，一時間掀起了一陣"聖誕節過還是不過"的爭議。往後每年聖誕來臨之際，常有土洋交鋒。

我跟朋友聊到洋節在中國流行的原因時，朋友的說法頗有代表性。他說，在生活節奏日益緊張的今天，借著洋節的名，約幾個朋友聚聚，天南海北侃侃，釋放壓力，加深友情，交流信息，換來一個好心情，何樂而不為？不知道那些洋節的來歷又有何妨？對老百姓來說，甭管是洋節、土節，只要讓人過得開心就行。另外，我發現，國人過洋節的那份狂熱，還應該歸功於商家的推波助瀾。最典型的要數聖誕節了，商家通過渲染節日氣氛，推出一系列聖誕優惠購物活動，激起消費欲望，然後大賺一筆。最后，還有一個原因恐怕跟文化優勢有關。不要說我們的土節，就是佛教、伊斯蘭教的節日也同樣敵不過基督教背景的聖誕節。這倒不是說中國人對基督教更認同，而是聖誕節讓人聯想到的是歐美發達國家的生活方式，在普通老百姓眼裡代表的是一種富裕、悠閑的生活方式，作為一個老百姓，誰不希望自己能跟富裕的文明靠近一點呢？

　　一些學者認為，不同的地理、文化、歷史、風俗習慣造就了不同國家的節日，但這並不妨礙人們在節日上互通有無。節日作為文化的一部分，應該是兼容並蓄的。舉個例子來說，我們的父母為我們辛苦操勞，養育之恩無以回報，因而在"父親節"、"母親節"特別為父母做一件事，表達一份心意，應該是一件很值得肯定的事，過這樣的洋節不是更能弘揚中華民族尊老敬老的傳統美德嗎？其他一些節日，比如聖誕節，如果能讓人們在這些節日相互祝福、與親朋好友共度一段閒暇時光，也是無可厚非的。還有諸如愚人節、萬聖節之類單純用來消遣和娛樂的洋節，給大家開玩笑的借口、穿得奇形怪狀的機會，給一成不變的生活增加點亮色，何樂而不為？在某些人眼裡，過洋節就是崇洋媚外的標志。實際上，在這樣一個全球化的時代，非議過洋節，或者想把某種文化拒之門外，是不切實際的，也是沒有必要的；更好的辦法是借助逐漸強大的國力，將自己的傳統文化推向世界，在與別國文化的交流和碰撞中，尋求傳統文化的立足點，並以此豐富世界文化。

　　也有人指出，洋節的興起與我們目前思想的開放、追求生活方式的西化、對西方文化的盲從是分不開的。不錯，洋節在某種程度上是我們了解外國風情、了解世界各族文化的窗口。可洋節畢竟是洋人的節日，中國人過洋節，往往過的是洋節的"皮"，根本不知道"瓤"是什麼。2月14日給女朋友送999朵玫瑰，卻不知丘比特是誰；聖誕之夜又蹦又跳地去搶禮物，可連耶穌的來歷都還沒搞清，這樣的人大有人在。說到聖誕節，那是個宗教節日，要是你一不看《圣经》，二不做禮拜，過哪門子聖誕呀！從深層來講，過洋節其實是弱勢民族在追求現代化過程中對強勢民族的一種仿效行為。我們中國有自己的民族文化，而且絕不是一種劣等文化。對那些洋節，我們應該說"不"。

　　還有一位學者在接受記者採訪時表示，我們不應該簡單地拒絕"洋節"，因為外來節日充實了我們的文化生活；當然也絕不能丟棄自己的節日，因為傳統節日是民族文化的精髓，如果毀棄，是對歷史的不負責任。同時，傳統節日也是傳承文化最好的載體。在全球化的時代，世界正變得越來越雷同，這時候，民族文化往往是最值得珍惜的資源。因此，我們要重視和保護我們的傳統，並把它發揚光大。

新词语

洋	洋	yáng	foreign ~人/~货/~房/~文; 反义词, 土 local; native 土产/土著; unfashionable 打扮得很土; stupid and clumsy 土头土脑

青睐	青睞	qīnglài	to favor; to like 公司~有技能的人/他的作品无人~
万圣节	萬聖節	Wànshèngjié	Halloween 10 月 31 日~晚上孩子们喜欢打扮得像鬼一样, 挨家挨户要糖果/孩子在~用南瓜做灯笼
情人节	情人節	Qíngrénjié	Valentine's Day 浪漫的~礼物
愚人节	愚人節	Yúrénjié	April Fools' Day 4 月 1 日~有些人喜欢愚弄容易受骗上当的人/一个~的玩笑
如数家珍	如數家珍	rú shǔ jiā zhēn	to be very familiar with one's subject; literally, as if enumerating one's family treasures 谈起公司的情况, 他~/提起足球员, 他~
具体	具體	jùtǐ	concrete; specific ~计划/~建议/~影响/~时间
寥寥无几	寥寥無幾	liáo liáo wú jǐ	to be very few in number; 数量很少 来看演出的人~/工作机会~
抵制	抵制	dǐzhì	to resist; to boycott; 抵抗制止 ~不好的影响/~诱惑 (yòuhuò temptation)/~外国货/~这次会议
抵御	抵禦	dǐyù	to defend against; 抵抗防御 ~敌人/~疾病/~危机/~寒冷/~网络的不良影响
倡议书	倡議書	chàngyìshū	written proposal 发出~/签署~
掀起	掀起	xiānqǐ	to stir up; to raise ~研究中国问题的热潮/汽车经过, ~大量尘土/~面罩/~锅盖
来临之际	來臨之際	lái lín zhī jì	to be approaching; 将要到来的时候 母亲节~/春天~/暴风雨~
交锋	交鋒	jiāofēng	to contend for in rivalry; contest; 交: to cross; 锋: the cutting edge of a sword 两校篮球队即将~/思想的~使辩论十分生动
颇	頗	pō	quite 影响~大/~受欢迎
代表性	代表性	dàibiǎoxìng	typical; representative 西安最有~的小吃是羊肉泡馍/韩非子是法家的~人物
节奏	節奏	jiézòu	rhythm 快~的生活/音乐的~/~感
侃	侃	kǎn	to chat idly; to chatter; 闲聊; 无边无际地聊 几个人在一起~上了/什么话题他都能胡~
释放	釋放	shìfàng	to relieve; to release 把压力~出来/透过舞蹈~感情/犯人被~了/核电厂 (hé diànchǎng nuclear power plant) 出事以后~出大量辐射 (fúshè radiation)
甭	甭	béng	don't; 不用 ~紧张/~怕他
狂热	狂熱	kuángrè	fanaticism; ardent; madly 宗教~/~的电影迷/~地爱上了她
推波助澜	推波助瀾	tuī bō zhù lán	to add fuel to the fire; to make a stormy sea stormier; 澜: 大波浪 他不但不调解那两人的争执, 反而~/这只是件小事, 别~, 否则会变成大事
典型	典型	diǎnxíng	typical; 有代表性 ~的中国人/感冒~的症状是感觉疲倦
渲染	渲染	xuànrǎn	to exaggerate; to play up; 中国画技法的一种, 以水墨或淡彩涂染画面, 增加艺术效果 他们的故事被过分~/有些记者喜欢~新闻

激起	激起	jīqǐ	to arouse; 激发 ~兴趣/~食欲/~对文学的热爱/这些问题~他的好奇心
消费	消费	xiāofèi	to consume; consumption 有的人很少~, 他们把钱存起来/她限制自己的~
欲望	慾望	yùwàng	desire 发财的~/求知的~/强烈的~/求胜的~
悠闲	悠閒	yōuxián	leisurely and carefree; 从容无所牵挂 一副~的样子/~的日子/过得很~
造就	造就	zàojiù	to nurture; 培养成功; 培育 ~人才/艰苦的环境~了吃苦耐劳的人
互通有无	互通有無	hù tōng yǒu wú	each supplies what the other needs; 进行交换, 得到自己所没有的 我们的交流原则是平等互利, ~
兼容并蓄	兼容並蓄	jiān róng bìng xù	to embrace things of different natures; 把不同的东西收留下来、保存起来 中西文化~没有一种理论是完美的, 将各种理论~, 取长补短, 才是办法
操劳	操勞	cāoláo	to work hard; 辛苦地劳动 为孩子~/~了一辈子
回报	回報	huíbào	to repay; something given in return; 报答 ~社会/~他对我的帮助/期望~/金钱~
心意	心意	xīnyì	small token of gratitude; kindness; heart's desire 这礼物是我的一点儿~/你的~, 我们领情了/我无法改变孩子的~
弘扬	弘扬	hóngyáng	to carry forward; to promote ~中国文化/~男女平等的观念
美德	美德	měidé	virtue 传统~/节俭的~/具有~
共度	共度	gòngdù	to spend time together 与家人~周末/夫妻~一生
闲暇	閒暇	xiánxiá	free time; spare time; 空闲的时间 利用周末~的时间/在工作的~谈天
消遣	消遣	xiāoqiǎn	to pass the time by doing something that gives one delight; pastime; 做感兴趣的事情来打发时间 到酒吧、歌厅~/唱歌~/活动/把读小说当作~
崇洋媚外	崇洋媚外	chóng yáng mèi wài	to worship everything foreign and to be subservient to foreigners; 崇拜西方, 巴结外国人 有的人~/~的心理
非议	非議	fēiyì	to reproach; censure; 批评; 责难 遭到~/受到~/引来~/一些~
不切实际	不切實際	bú qiè shíjì	unrealistic or impractical 他的想法~/~的目标
碰撞	碰撞	pèngzhuàng	clash; to clash 发生~/两辆车~在一起
立足点	立足點	lìzúdiǎn	foothold; 立脚点; 基地 我们在欧洲市场已经有了稳定的~/他帮我的公司在纽约设立了一个
盲从	盲從	mángcóng	to follow blindly 对什么事情都不能~/别~朋友
风情	風情	fēngqíng	customs and practices; charm 外国的~/这座古城的~/西藏的民俗~带有东方~/浪漫~/这个女人喜欢卖弄~
瓤	瓤	ráng	pulp; 果肉 西瓜~/橘子~
蹦	蹦	bèng	to hop; to jump; to bounce ~~跳跳/~来~去/~起来/~上床/在床上~/在沙发上~

耶稣	耶穌	yēsū	Jesus ~是上帝的儿子
圣经	聖經	shèngjīng	the Bible 有人说, ~是一部伟大的文学作品
做礼拜	做禮拜	zuòlǐbài	to go to church 基督教徒(jīdū jiàotú Protestants) ~, 天主教徒 (tiānzhǔ jiàotú Catholics) 望弥撒 (wàng mísā to attend Mass)
弱势	弱勢	ruòshì	weak; underprivileged ~群体/~百姓
强势	強勢	qiángshì	powerful; aggressive 她有~的一面, 也有软弱的一面/他说话的口气太~, 让人听起来很不舒服
仿效	仿效	fǎngxiào	to follow the example of; to model oneself after someone; to imitate; 模仿 ~美国/~父母/有的女孩喜欢~电影明星
劣等	劣等	lièděng	of inferior quality; poor; 低等; 下等 ~货/~生/~作品/~成绩
充实	充實	chōngshí	to enrich; to expand one's horizons; fulfilling ~生活/~自己/~的生活
丢弃	丢棄	diūqì	to discard; to abandon ~旧衣服/~垃圾/~自己的母语/被~的汽车
精髓	精髓	jīngsuí	essence 京剧的~/思想的~
毁弃	毀棄	huǐqì	to destroy ~证据/珍贵的资料遭到~
传承	傳承	chuánchéng	to pass on; 传播、继承 让传统文化代代~/~少数民族艺术
载体	載體	zàitǐ	transmitter; vehicle; 传递的工具 语言是文化的~/古诗词是传统文化的~
全球化	全球化	quánqiúhuà	globalization 市场~/业务~
雷同	雷同	léitóng	exactly the same 风格~/~的产品
珍惜	珍惜	zhēnxī	to cherish ~时间/~生命
资源	資源	zīyuán	resource ~丰富/~不足/石油 (shíyóu petroleum) ~/人才~
发扬光大	發揚光大	fā yáng guāng dà	to develop and cause to shine forth; to make flourish 使优良传统~/让中国文化~

重点词语和句式

1 最······莫过于······ (the most . . . is none other than)

(1) 网络上、媒体上关于"洋节"、"土节"的辩论随处可见。最引人注目的莫过于 2006 年 12 月 10 名中国名校的博士联名发出的抵制圣诞节、抵御西方文化扩张的倡议书。

(Everywhere on the internet and in the news media, we could read and see debates between people who were in favor of Western holidays and people who were in favor of native holidays. What attracted our attention the most was none other than the written proposal by ten Ph.D.s from famous Chinese universities in December 2006 to boycott Christmas and defend China against the spread of Western culture.)

(2) 在中国, 最重要的节日莫过于春节。
(In China, the most important holiday is none other than the Spring Festival.)

(3) A: 在北美大学, 最难的课是什么?
(In North American universities, what is the most difficult course?)

B: 在我们大学, 最难的课莫过于经济学课。
(At our university, the most difficult course is none other than economics.)

用"最……莫过于……"完成句子:

(1) 我经常看电影, 最喜欢的电影莫过于_____

(2) 去中国旅游, 给我印象最深刻的莫过于_____

2 借着……的名 (借……之名) (to use something as an excuse or a pretext; under the pretense of)

(1) [我们]借着洋节的名, 约几个朋友聚聚。
(We use Western holidays as excuses to invite a few friends over for parties.)

(2) 有人说政府不能借反恐之名限制人们的自由。
(Some people say that the government cannot use the fight against terrorism as a pretext for restricting citizens' freedom.)

(3) 有的人借着找对象的名, 骗财骗色。
(Under the pretense of searching for mates, some swindlers coaxed money and sex from women.)

用"借着……的名 (借……之名) "完成句子:

(1) 有的人借着工作的名,_____

(2) 虽然你是名校的学生, 你别借着名校之名_____

3 何乐而不为 (Why not do it? It's worth doing; 这么快乐为什么不做?)

(1) 天南海北侃侃, ……换来一个好心情, 何乐而不为?
([We] chat about everything imaginable . . . and are in good moods. Why shouldn't we [celebrate Western holidays]?)

(2) A: 你家旁边就是购物中心, 你为什么一定要在网上买东西呢?
(There is a shopping mall right next to your home. Why do you have to shop online?)

B: 网上购物又方便又便宜, 还能节省时间, 何乐而不为?
(Shopping online is convenient, cheap and also saves time. Why not do it?)

(3) A: 你有车, 为什么要骑自行车呢?
(You have a car. Why do you ride a bike?)

B: 骑自行车又环保又锻炼身体, 何乐而不为?
(Riding a bike is good for both the environment and the body. It's worth doing.)

用"何乐而不为"完成对话:

(1) A: 情人节你给女朋友已经送了巧克力, 为什么又送鲜花?

   B: _____

(2) A: 蔬菜那么便宜, 干嘛还花时间种?

   B: _____

4 又有何妨 (*yòu yǒu hé fáng* 妨: 阻碍; 伤害; to hamper; to harm; [although] . . . what does it matter/what harm is there? 又有什么关系? 又有什么不好?)

(1) 借着洋节的名, 约几个朋友聚聚, 天南海北侃侃, ……换来一个好心情, 何乐而不为? 不知道那些洋节的来历又有何妨?
   (We use Western holidays as excuses to invite a few friends over for parties. We chat about everything imaginable . . . and are in good moods. Why shouldn't we celebrate [Western holidays]? What does it matter that we don't know their origins?)

(2) A: 我很喜欢那个男人, 可是我不敢跟他说话, 也许他已经有女朋友了。
   (I like that man, but I don't dare talk to him. Maybe he already has a girlfriend.)

   B: 你去跟他说说话又有何妨?
   (What harm is there in just talking with him?)

(3) A: 那个工作我很喜欢, 可是要求很高, 我不敢去申请。
   (I like that job, but it requires high qualifications. I don't dare apply for it.)

   B: 你试试又有何妨?
   (What harm is there in trying?)

翻译:

(1) I know that you have broken up with your boyfriend, but what harm would there be in having coffee together?

   _____

(2) A: I can't dance anymore. I'm exhausted.

   _____

   B: What harm is there in one more dance?

   _____

5 归功于 (*guī gōng yú* to owe to; to attribute the success [of something] to)

(1) 国人过洋节的那份狂热, 还应该归功于商家的推波助澜。
   (The fervor with which Chinese celebrate Western holidays owes a great deal to the businesses' vigorous promotion.)

(2) 他把自己在钢琴演奏上的成功归功于父亲。
   (He attributes his success as a concert pianist to his father.)

(3) 他在比赛中能得到金牌, 要归功于他持之以恒的练习。

(He attributes his winning the gold medal in the competition to his relentless training.)

用"归功于"完成句子:

(1) 比尔·盖茨的成功要归功于 _____

(2) 苹果公司的产品受到年轻人的青睐要归功于 _____

6 要数⋯⋯了 (probably)

(1) 国人过洋节的那份狂热, 还应该归功于商家的推波助澜。最典型的要数圣诞节了。

(The fervor with which the Chinese celebrate Western holidays owes a great deal to the businesses' vigorous promotion. Christmas is probably a typical example.)

(2) 在中国, 最重要的节日要数春节了。

(In China, the most important holiday is probably the Spring Festival.)

(3) 冰淇淋的口味很多, 最普通的要数香草和巧克力了。

(There are many flavors of ice cream. The most common are probably vanilla and chocolate.)

用"要数⋯⋯了"完成句子:

(1) 我最喜欢的中国菜 / 电影 / 演员 / 地方要数 _____ 了。

(2) 对学生来说, 最忙最累的日子要数 _____ 了。

7 不要说⋯⋯, 就是⋯⋯也⋯⋯ (literally, to say nothing of [something or someone] . . . even . . . also . . .; not to mention)

(1) 不要说我们的土节, 就是佛教、伊斯兰教的节日也同样敌不过基督教背景的圣诞节。

(Holidays of Buddhist and Islamic origin—to say nothing of our own native holidays—are no match for the Christian Christmas.)

(2) 现在经济不好, 不要说低收入的家庭, 就是一些中产家庭也都开始想办法赚钱。

(Times are bad now. Some middle-class families have started to look for ways to save, to say nothing of low-income families.)

(3) 他是个辛劳的医生, 不要说周末, 就是公共假期也看病。

(He is a hardworking doctor. He sees patients on public holidays, not to mention weekends.)

用"不要说⋯⋯就是⋯⋯也⋯⋯"完成对话:

(1) A: 你是老师, 这个难题, 学生能回答吗?

  B: _____

(2) A: 他破产以后, 我借给了他许多钱, 但是他还是不断要求我帮助他。

  B: _____

8 敌不过 (to be no match for; unable to hold out against or withstand; unable to survive)

(1) 不要说我们的土节，佛教、伊斯兰教的节日也同样敌不过基督教背景的圣诞节。
(Holidays of Buddhist and Islamic origin—to say nothing of our own native holidays—are no match for the Christian Christmas.)

(2) "寡不敌众"的意思就是少数敌不过多数。
(The saying "the few are no match for the many" means that the minority cannot hold out against the majority.)

(3) 二十年的婚姻敌不过一个星期的婚外情。
(Even a twenty-year-long marriage cannot survive a week-long extramarital affair.)

翻译：

(1) The United States men's national basketball team often wins. The Chinese men's national team is no match for them.

_____

(2) He said that he would love her forever, but their love could not withstand the test of time.

_____

9 倒不是 (it doesn't mean that; not necessarily so)

(1) ……这倒不是说中国人对基督教更认同，而是圣诞节让人联想到的是欧美发达国家的生活方式。
(. . . This doesn't mean that the Chinese believe in Christianity. Instead, Christmas reminds them of the lifestyle in developed European countries.)

(2) 他破产了，他倒不是笨，只是运气不好。
(Just because he's bankrupt doesn't necessarily mean he's stupid. He's only unlucky.)

(3) A: 你不去那个舞会，是不是怕碰见你的前男友？
(You don't want to go to that dance. Is it because you're afraid of bumping into your ex-boyfriend?)

B: 我倒不是怕碰见他，我不去是因为没有时间。
(It isn't necessarily that I'm afraid of bumping into him. It's just that I have no time.)

用"倒不是"完成对话：

A: 你现在改骑自行车，是为了省钱吗？

B: _____

翻译：

I can't stop listening to that song. It's not that I like the song; it's that it reminds me of her.

_____

10 无以 (cannot do something; 没有什么可以用来……)

(1) 我们的父母为我们辛苦操劳, 养育之恩无以回报。
(Our parents work hard for us. We cannot ever repay them for their love and care.)

(2) 他问我怎样发财, 面对这样的问题, 我无以回答。
(He asked me how to get rich. To such a question, I had no reply.)

(3) 感激你给我的帮助, 实在无以表达谢意。
(I'm grateful for your help. I truly cannot express my gratitude.)

翻译:

(1) He criticizes me for no good reason. Words cannot express my anger.

_____

(2) His parents want him to become a doctor. He has no choice.

_____

11 无可厚非 (to give no cause for criticism; justifiable; 没有什么好过分批评、责备的)

(1) 如果能让人们在这些节日相互祝福、与亲朋好友共度一段闲暇时光, 也是无可厚非的。
(If these holidays allow people to wish each other well and spend some leisure time with relatives and good friends, we cannot hold anything against them.)

(2) 谁都有爱美之心, 女人做整容手术也无可厚非。
(Everyone wants to be beautiful. We cannot criticize these women for undergoing plastic surgery.)

(3) 她认为要达到目标, 使用任何手段都无可厚非。
(She thinks that it is justifiable to use any means to reach her goal.)

翻译:

(1) A: Why aren't his children studying?

_____

B: Little children like to play. We can't find fault with that.

_____

(2) That old man worked hard all his life. It is only right that he enjoys his life now.

_____

12 诸如……之类 (such as [this type of])

(1) 还有诸如愚人节、万圣节之类单纯用来消遣和娱乐的洋节, 给大家开玩笑的借口、穿得奇形怪状的机会, 给一成不变的生活增加点亮色, 何乐而不为?
(For pure enjoyment and entertainment, there are other Western holidays such as April Fools' Day and Halloween. If these holidays allow people to play practical

jokes, wear strange costumes, and add color to their dull lives, why shouldn't we celebrate them?)

(2) 有些孩子忙于诸如舞蹈、音乐、体育之类的课外活动。
(Some children are busy with extracurricular activities such as dance, music, and sports.)

(3) 很少人喜欢做诸如烧饭、洗衣之类的事情。
(Few people like to do chores such as cooking and doing laundry.)

翻译:

(1) I like classical Chinese novels such as *Water Margin* and *Dream of the Red Chamber*.

_____

(2) We didn't have a serious talk. We only chatted about subjects like the weather and sports.

_____

13 A与B是分不开的 (A can be explained by B; A is a result of B; A is inextricably linked to B)

(1) 洋节的兴起, 与我们目前思想的开放、从众的心理、追求生活方式的西化、对西方文化的盲从是分不开的。
(The rise in popularity of Western holidays can be explained by our present open-mindedness, our desire to conform, our pursuit of the Western way of life, and our blind adoption of Western culture.)

(2) 他的成功与他的努力是分不开的。
(His success is a result of his hard work.)

(3) 教育很重要, 一个国家的前途与人民的教育是分不开的。
(Education is important. A country's future is inextricably linked to the education of its people.)

用"A与B是分不开的"完成对话:

(1) A: 他成功地跑完了马拉松, 你认为他的毅力重要吗?

B: _____

(2) A: 人要活得快乐, 健康重要还是金钱重要?

B: _____

14 在某种程度上 (to some extent; in some ways)

(1) 洋节在某种程度上是我们了解外国风情、了解世界各族文化的窗口。
(To some extent, Western holidays serve as windows through which we can understand the customs of foreign countries and the cultures of various ethnic groups.)

(2) 就业市场的激烈竞争, 在某种程度上改变了人们的就业观念。

(In some ways, the fierce competition in the job market has changed people's ideas of acceptable work.)

(3) 目前的经济衰退在某种程度上改变了人们的消费习惯。

(In some ways, the current recession has changed people's habits of consumption.)

用"在某种程度上"完成对话:

(1) A: 孩子们再忙也应该做点儿家务事。

　　B: _____

(2) A: 你喜欢她吗? 她有点儿笨。

　　B: _____

15　大有人在 (there are plenty of people who . . .)

(1) 圣诞之夜又蹦又跳地去抢礼物, 可连耶稣的来历都还没搞清, 这样的人大有人在。

(There are plenty of people who jump at the opportunity to grab presents on Christmas Eve, but who don't even know who Jesus is.)

(2) 这房子真贵, 但买得起的中国人大有人在。

(This house is really expensive, but there are plenty of Chinese who could afford it.)

(3) 买卖股票可以发财, 有这样想法的老百姓大有人在。

(There are plenty of ordinary people who think that they can get rich by trading stocks.)

翻译:

(1) There are plenty of parents who agree that we should not spoil our children.

_____

(2) A: I don't like this politician.

_____

B: There are plenty of voters who do like him.

_____

16　一不……二不…… (number one, don't . . . and, number two, don't . . .; number one . . . isn't . . . and, number two, . . . isn't . . .)

(1) 要是你一不看《圣经》, 二不做礼拜, 过哪门子圣诞呀!

(If you, number one, don't read the Bible and, number two, don't go to church, what on earth are you celebrating Christmas for?)

(2) 我母亲认为他一不喝酒, 二不抽烟, 是个难得的好人。

(My mother thinks that he's an extraordinarily good man. Number one, he doesn't drink and, number two, he doesn't smoke.)

(3) 今天一不是假日，二不是谁的生日，怎么做这么多菜？
(Number one, today isn't a holiday and, number two, today isn't anyone's birthday. How come you have cooked so many dishes?)

翻译:

(1) A: How did you get this rich?

_____

  B: Number one, I didn't steal and, number two, I didn't rob. I've made my money the honest way.

_____

(2) A: Should we still go to the movies? It's raining outside.

_____

  B: Let me tell you why we should still go. Number one, I'm not tired and, number two, I'm not busy. What does a little rain matter?

_____

练习

一. 根据课文, 回答问题

(1) 请介绍一下洋节在中国流行的原因。
(2) "土洋交锋"双方各有哪些说法？
(3) 我们能不拒绝"洋节"也不抛弃"土节"吗？

二. 用以下每题所给的词语或句式完成对话

(1) A: 洋节、土节你喜欢过哪个？

  B: _____
  (最……莫过于 借着 何乐而不为)

(2) A: 为什么有的中国人爱过圣诞节？

  B: _____
  (归功于 渲染 激起)

(3) A: 为什么我们在节日上应该互通有无、兼容并蓄？

  B: _____
  (诸如……之类 弘扬 无可厚非)

(4) A: 为什么有人说中国人过的是洋节的"皮"？

  B: _____
  (在某种程度上 大有人在 哪门子)

(5) A: 中国人有自己的文化、自己的节日。

　　B: _____

　　(一不……, 二不…… 无以 珍惜)

三. 根据所给的情景完成对话, 尽量用本课所学的新词语, 请在新词语下面划出一道线

(1) 圣诞节快到了, 已经工作的儿子想跟父亲借钱给朋友们买礼物, 父亲不理解他为什么要过圣诞节。父子两个人的对话会说些什么?

(2) 老张去商店买东西, 看到圣诞节购物优惠的广告到处都是, 感到很不理解。碰见老朋友老王 (老王是这家商店的老板) 后, 两个人会说些什么呢?

(3) 小赵是发出抵制圣诞节倡议书的十位博士之一。他跟他的记者朋友小刘一起聊天, 谈到发倡议书这件事时, 他们会说些什么?

四. 写作练习

在北美, 你们过什么节? 你对中国人过这些洋节, 有什么看法? 题目自己决定, 字数: 500–700 字。

五. 辩论

题目: 中国人应不应该过洋节?
正方: 中国人应该过洋节
反方: 中国人不应该过洋节
辩论的内容可以考虑以下方面:

　　(1) 过洋节是不是崇洋媚外?
　　(2) 各个国家的节日可不可以互通有无?
　　(3) 过洋节是不是了解外国文化的窗口?
　　(4) 中国人过洋节是不是"不伦不类"?
　　(5) 洋节在中国流行是不是一种商业行为的结果?
　　(6) 全球化与保护文化遗产是不是矛盾的?

第8课　星巴克引发的争议

Figure 8.1 星巴克进驻故宫
by Mingming Cheung (2020)

© Mingming Cheung.

Figure 8.2 宫女在宫装外面穿上比基尼
by Mingming Cheung (2020)

© Mingming Cheung.

Figure 8.3 故宫拉面每碗¥30
by Mingming Cheung (2020)

© Mingming Cheung.

Figure 8.4 星巴克在灵隐寺开店
by Mingming Cheung (2020)

© Mingming Cheung.

　　2000年10月, 被很多人认为象征西方商业文化的美国连锁店星巴克进驻具有近六百年历史的故宫。从那时起, 争论之声就不绝于耳。争论集中在两个焦点问题: 第一、象征全球化的星巴克咖啡是否有侵犯中国五千年文化之嫌; 第二、星巴克的招牌是否和代表中国传统文化的故宫形成冲突。

　　很多人认为在故宫销售外国的东西或出现外国的广告, 感觉上不伦不类。星巴克开在故宫, 好比宫女在宫装外面穿上比基尼一样让人别扭。所以说, 这不是全球化, 而是西方文化对中国文化的侵蚀, 是两种文化的对抗。还有人说, 在故宫里看到星巴克, 很容易就联想到了八国联军。假如真的要卖喝的, 那就卖点儿茶。洋人想喝咖啡的话, 可以到别处喝, 不一定非要在故宫喝。

　　在故宫星巴克喝过咖啡的美国人艾丽斯表示, 故宫有个星巴克是件好事, 尤其是在寒冷的冬天, 游客能喝杯热咖啡或是热巧克力, 真是舒服极了, 而且这对故宫来说也是一个很好的商业机会。艾丽斯认为, 故宫星巴克实在是不值得争论的事情, 真要关注的应该是如何去维护北京那些几百年传下来的建筑。艾丽斯说: "北京现在已经面目全非, 有保存价值的古建筑几乎都拆光了, 取而代之的净是些灵气全无、喧宾夺主的大型现代建筑。我要是北京人的话, 会对这个事实更加焦虑。"

　　一位学者说, 如果当年法国密特朗总统出于狭隘的民族主义心态, 不邀请美籍华人贝聿铭设计法国卢浮宫广场, 也就没有今天卢浮广场的玻璃金字塔了。故宫星巴克这种本不值得大惊小怪的商业服务闹成这么大的新闻, 这里面有一种强烈的民族主义的情结, 是小题大做。我们有这么悠久的传统, 难道一小杯咖啡就可以把我们打倒吗? 改革开放这么多年, 我们追求的包容又在哪里呢?

　　另一位历史学家表示支持星巴克撤出故宫。他指出, 历史就是一面镜子。忘记历史就等于背叛过去, 包容西方文化并不等于要忘记历史。故宫曾经被八国联军占领过, 故宫里的星巴克恰恰勾起了中国人对近代屈辱历史的痛苦回忆。没有任何理由要求中国人忘记这段历史, 正如不能要求美国人忘记珍珠港事件、日本人忘记广岛和长崎的原子弹爆炸、犹太人忘记奥斯威辛集中营一样。包容他者不等于放弃自我, 否则就不是包容而是投降了。事实上, 任何包容都是有限度的, 一味模仿甚至原样照抄就会成为邯郸学步。在经历了百余年激烈的反传统之后, 中国文化的象征性场所已是所剩无几, 长城、孔庙、故宫等正是最后的文化象征。中国人把自己的文化情怀、民族自尊投射于这些文化场所, 希望它们保持古色古香和民族特色, 自然是无可非议的。

2007年7月，在舆论的压力和网民的抗议之下，已开设了七年之久的星巴克咖啡从故宫正式撤出。

星巴克撤出故宫让那些以传统文化保护者自居的人们兴奋了一阵子。但接下来进驻故宫的原汁原味的本土拉面，又因其每碗30元的高价引起了公众的强烈批评。其实，不管故宫是卖星巴克咖啡，还是卖中国拉面，这里面还涉及到另一个更敏感的问题，那就是故宫这样的文化象征应不应该商业化。

故宫之争平息不久，2012年9月，星巴克在杭州灵隐寺景区开店，随之再次引发新的争议。星巴克灵隐门店并非在灵隐寺内，而是在灵隐寺景区的游客服务区内。有人对此表示理解，认为景区管理机构为了提升灵隐寺的商业价值，引入星巴克似乎无可厚非。另一部分人则持反对的态度，认为让名胜古迹染上了铜臭气。

如何在文化传统和商业开发之间寻找平衡点，一直是中国许多名胜古迹面临的难题。星巴克在故宫开店被认定是一种文化侵略，侵蚀了中国传统文化。星巴克在灵隐景区开店再次导致文化入侵之忧，也是因为看简单了它是一杯咖啡，看复杂了它是一个文化符号。对这个问题的争议恐怕不会一朝一夕就能得出结论。

(第三自然段引自"美国之音"的"紫禁城内星巴克去留再成争论焦点"，2007年1月18日 www.voachinese.com/a/a-21-w2007-01-18-voa37-63061952/1045834.html)

第8課　星巴克引發的爭議

2000年10月，被很多人認為象徵西方商業文化的美國連鎖店星巴克進駐具有近六百年歷史的故宫。從那時起，爭論之聲就不絕於耳。爭論集中在兩個焦點問題：第一、象徵全球化的星巴克咖啡是否有侵犯中國五千年文化之嫌；第二、星巴克的招牌是否和代表中國傳統文化的故宫形成衝突。

很多人認為在故宫銷售外國的東西或出現外國的廣告，感覺上不倫不類。星巴克開在故宫，好比宮女在宮裝外面穿上比基尼一樣讓人彆扭。所以說，這不是全球化，而是西方文化對中國文化的侵蝕，是兩種文化的對抗。還有人說，在故宫裡看到星巴克，很容易就聯想到了八國聯軍。假如真的要賣喝的，那就賣點兒茶。洋人想喝咖啡的話，可以到別處喝，不一定非要在故宫喝。

在故宫星巴克喝過咖啡的美國人艾麗絲表示，故宫有個星巴克是件好事，尤其是在寒冷的冬天，遊客能喝杯熱咖啡或是熱巧克力,真是舒服極了,而且這對故宮來說也是一個很好的商業機會。艾麗絲認為,故宮星巴克實在是不值得爭論的事情,真要關注的應該是如何去維護北京那些幾百年傳下來的建築。艾麗絲說:"北京現在已經面目全非,有保存價值的建築幾乎都拆光了,取而代之的淨是些靈氣全無、喧賓奪主的大型建築。我要是北京人的話,會對這個事實更加焦慮。"

一位學者說,如果當年法國密特朗總統出於狹隘的民族主義心態,不邀請美籍華人貝聿銘設計法國盧浮宮廣場,也就沒有今天盧浮廣場的玻璃金字塔了。故宮星巴克這種本不值得大驚小怪的商業服務鬧成這麼大的新聞,這裡面有一種強烈的民族主義的情結,是小題大做。我們有這麼悠久的傳統,難道一小杯咖啡就可以把我們打倒嗎?改革開放這麼多年,我們追求的包容又在哪裡呢?

另一位歷史學家表示支持星巴克撤出故宮。他指出,歷史就是一面鏡子。忘記歷史就等於背叛過去,包容西方文化並不等於要忘記歷史。故宮曾經被八國聯軍佔領過,故宮裡的星巴克恰恰勾起了中國人對近代屈辱歷史的痛苦回憶。沒有任何理由要求中國人忘記這段歷史,正如不能要求美國人忘記珍珠港事件、日本人忘記廣島和長崎的原子彈爆炸、猶太人忘記奧斯威辛集中營一樣。包容他者不等於放棄自我,否則就不是包容而是投降了。事實上,任何包容都是有限度的,一味模仿甚至原樣照抄就會成為邯鄲學步。在經歷了百餘年激烈的反傳統之後,中國文化的象徵性場所已是所剩無幾,長城、孔廟、故宮等正是最後的文化象徵。中國人把自己的文化情懷、民族自尊投射於這些文化場所,希望它們保持古色古香和民族特色,自然是無可非議的。

2007年7月,在輿論的壓力和網民的抗議之下,已開設了七年之久的星巴克咖啡從故宮正式撤出。

星巴克撤出故宮讓那些以傳統文化保護者自居的人們興奮了一陣子。但接下來進駐故宮的原汁原味的本土拉麵,又因其每碗30元的高價引起了公眾的強烈批評。其實,不管故宮是賣星巴克咖啡,還是賣中國拉麵,這裡面還涉及到另一個更敏感的問題,那就是故宮這樣的文化象徵應不應該商業化。

故宮之爭平息不久,2012年9月,星巴克在杭州靈隱寺景區開店,隨之再次引發新的爭議。星巴克靈隱門店並非在靈隱寺內,而是在靈隱寺景區的遊客服務區內。有人對此表示理解,認為景區管理機構為了提升靈隱寺的商業價值,引入星巴克似乎無可厚非。另一部分人則持反對的態度,認為讓名勝古跡染上了銅臭氣。

如何在文化傳統和商業開發之間尋找平衡點，一直是中國許多名勝古跡面臨的難題。星巴克在故宮開店被認定是一種文化侵略，侵蝕了中國傳統文化。星巴克在靈隱景區開店再次導致文化入侵之憂，也是因為看簡單了它是一杯咖啡，看複雜了它是一個文化符號。對這個問題的爭議恐怕不會一朝一夕就能得出結論。

(第三自然段引自"美國之音"的"紫禁城內星巴克去留再成爭論焦点"，2007年1月18日 www.voachinese.com/a/a-21-w2007-01-18-voa37-63061952/1045834.html)

新词语

星巴克	星巴克	Xīngbākè	Starbucks ~分店
争议	爭議	zhēngyì	controversy; controversial; dispute 产生~/避开有~的问题/有关版权的~
连锁店	連鎖店	liánsuǒdiàn	chain store 快餐~/旅馆~
进驻	進駐	jìnzhù	(of troops) to enter and be stationed in 军队~小镇/知名品牌~购物城
不绝于耳	不絕於耳	bù jué yú ěr	(of sound) to remain vibrating in the ears; 在耳边不停地响 反对之声~
集中	集中	jízhōng	to center upon; focused 母亲把精力~在孩子身上/我们注意力不够~
侵犯	侵犯	qīnfàn	to invade; to infringe upon ~别的国家/~知识产权
冲突	衝突	chōngtū	conflict 发生~/文化~/暴力~
销售	銷售	xiāoshòu	to sell; sale ~商品/特价~
广告	廣告	guǎnggào	advertisement 在电视上做~/报纸上的~
不伦不类	不倫不類	bù lún bú lèi	neither fish nor fowl; 既不是这一类，也不是那一类 非驴非马，~，四不像
宫女	宮女	gōngnǚ	lady-in-waiting 古代~
比基尼	比基尼	bǐjīní	bikini ~泳装
侵蚀	侵蝕	qīnshí	erosion; to erode; 逐渐侵害 森林可以抵御风沙的~/经过多年风雨的~，石碑 (shíbēi stone tablet) 上的字已经模糊不清了/我们的友谊经得起岁月的~/土地受到~/老年人的利益~/~大家的健康
对抗	對抗	duìkàng	confrontation; to resist; 这两国关系紧张，可能会有军事~/阿拉伯国家和以色列的~/~敌人/~感冒
联想	聯想	liánxiǎng	to associate in the mind; 因为一件事想起另一件事 听到那首歌就~到我的初恋/她说话的样子让我们~起她的母亲
八国联军	八國聯軍	Bāguó Liánjūn	Eight-Nation Alliance ~的八国是英、俄、日、法、德、美、意、奥/1900年~烧毁了圆明园

维护	維護	wéihù	to preserve; to save; to defend; 以行动、语言保护~世界和平/~他的好名声/~自己的权利
保存	保存	bǎocún	to preserve ~建筑古迹/把蔬菜水果~在冰箱里
拆	拆	chāi	to dismantle; to tear apart 旧房子~掉了/~开信封
净	淨	jìng	all the time; 总是 他~说假话/别~吃饭, 多吃菜
灵气	靈氣	língqì	aura; perceptive; 灵: 与神仙有关的; 形容像是仙人的地方; 形容人聪慧、灵敏 阳朔有山水之~/这个年轻人很有~
喧宾夺主	喧賓奪主	xuān bīn duó zhǔ	A presumptuous guest usurps the host's role; 客人谈论的声音超过了主人的声音, 比喻客人取代了主人的地位, 或是外来的、次要的事物侵占了原有的、主要的事物的地位; 喧: 大声吵嚷 在婚礼上, 那个花童~, 出尽风头, 大家都忘了新郎新娘
密特朗	密特朗	Mìtèlǎng	François Mitterrand 法国总统 (1981–1995)
狭隘	狹隘	xiá'ài	(of mind or knowledge) narrow; limited; 狭小 心胸~/~的观念
民族主义	民族主義	mínzú zhǔyì	nationalism 激进的~/强烈的~
心态	心態	xīntài	state of mind; 心理状态 良好的~/~不正常
贝聿铭	貝聿銘	Bèi Yùmíng	Leoh Ming Pei (1917–2019), commonly known as I.M. Pei, is a Chinese-born American architect.
卢浮宫	盧浮宮	Lúfú Gōng	the Louvre ~是巴黎最大的博物馆
广场	廣場	guǎngchǎng	public square 天安门~/古老小镇的~
玻璃	玻璃	bōlí	glass ~杯/~瓶/~窗
金字塔	金字塔	jīnzìtǎ	pyramid 古埃及大~
情结	情結	qíngjié	psychological or emotional complex; 心中的感情纠葛 (jiūgé entanglement) 自卑~/恋母~
小题大做	小题大做	xiǎo tí dà zuò	to handle a small case as if it were a big deal (implying a wasted effort); 科举时代, 考试题目从《四书》里出来的, 叫"小题", 从《五经》里出来的, 叫"大题," 以《五经》文章的章法来做《四书》的题目, 叫"小题大做"。以后比喻人把小事当作大事处理 这很常见, 你别~/为了这么小的事去找老师, 真是~
包容	包容	bāoróng	tolerance; to tolerate 完全的~/~别人的缺点
背叛	背叛	bèipàn	to betray ~朋友/~自己的誓言
恰恰	恰恰	qiàqià	exactly; precisely; 正好 你说的~是我想说的
勾起	勾起	gōuqǐ	to call to mind; to evoke; 引起 ~他的回忆/~食欲
屈辱	屈辱	qūrǔ	humiliated; humiliation; 委屈、耻辱 感到~/~的经历/受到许多~/忍受~
回忆	回憶	huíyì	memory; to recall 一段美好的~/~往事
珍珠港	珍珠港	Zhēnzhū Gǎng	Pearl Harbor 突袭~
广岛	廣島	Guǎngdǎo	Hiroshima 1945 年 8 月 6 日, 一颗原子弹投在日本的~
长崎	長崎	Chángqí	Nagasaki 1945 年 8 月 9 日, 一枚原子弹落在了~
原子弹	原子彈	yuánzǐdàn	nuclear bomb 引爆~

爆炸	爆炸	bàozhà	to explode 汽车~/炸弹~
犹太人	猶太人	Yóutàirén	Jewish person ~信犹太教
奥斯维辛	奧斯維辛	Àosīwéixīn	Auschwitz 波兰~的纳粹集中营
集中营	集中營	jízhōngyíng	concentration camp 战俘 (zhànfú prisoner of war)~
投降	投降	tóuxiáng	to surrender 向我们~/敌人~了
模仿	模仿	mófǎng	to imitate ~外国/他说话的样子/~老人走路
照抄	照抄	zhàochāo	to copy mechanically ~别人的做法/一字不变地~别人的著作
邯郸学步	邯郸学步	hándān xué bù	to imitate another person mechanically and lose one's own individuality;《庄子》里有个故事,战国时期,燕国Yānguó有个人到赵国的邯郸去,他看到邯郸的人走路姿势很漂亮,就跟着学,结果不但没有学好,连怎么走路也忘了,他爬着回去。后来比喻模仿他人,反而失去自己本来的面目一个人要有自己的个性,不能~/生硬地模仿只造成~
孔庙	孔廟	Kǒngmiào	Temple of Confucius 最早的~在山东曲阜Qūfù
情怀	情懷	qínghuái	feelings; 指某种心情、心境 浪漫~/怀旧~/中国~/爱国~
投射	投射	tóushè	to project; to cast; 把照片~在大屏幕上/那棵树的影子~在湖中
古色古香	古色古香	gǔ sè gǔ xiāng	in graceful ancient color and style ~的建筑/~的家具
抗议	抗議	kàngyì	protest; to protest 一场~/接二连三的~/~上街/~这件事情
撤	撤	chè	to withdraw; to evacuate; to remove 部队已经~到别的地点/由于地震,村子~空了/他被~了职
原汁原味	原汁原味	yuán zhī yuán wèi	original flavor, taste, or style ~的中国风格/这些菜~
本土	本土	běntǔ	one's native country or land ~品牌/~特色
拉面	拉麵	lāmiàn	fresh hand-pulled noodles 兰州牛肉~/上海炸酱~
敏感	敏感	mǐngǎn	sensitive ~的问题/他对这个话题很~
灵隐寺	靈隱寺	Língyǐn Sì	Temple of the Soul's Retreat ~有一千七百年的历史
景区	景區	jǐngqū	scenic area 旅游~/山林~
随之	隨之	suízhī	thereupon; subsequently 大雨过后,~出现了彩虹 (cǎihóng rainbow)/孩子打碎了花瓶,~吓得哭了起来
提升	提升	tíshēng	to raise; to advance; 提高 他的薪水~到一年二十万/他被~为经理
染	染	rǎn	to acquire (a bad habit); to catch (a virus or disease); to dye a color 他避免~上坏习惯/电脑~上了病毒/他~上了感冒/把头发~成了金黄色
铜臭气	銅臭氣	tóngxiù qì	the stink of copper coin; a term of ridicule applied to those who flaunt their wealth or seek nothing but profit 满身~/充满~
平衡点	平衡點	pínghéng diǎn	balance point 在工作和娱乐之间找到~/在两个极端之间找到~

面临	面臨	miànlín	to be confronted with; to be faced with; 面对 ~挑战/~压力
忧	憂	yōu	worry; to worry 衣食无~/时喜时~
符号	符號	fúhào	sign ~X表示未知数
一朝一夕	一朝一夕	yì zhāo yì xī	in one day; a short duration of time; literally, one morning and one night; 朝: 早; 夕: 晚 我有这个想法不是~了, 只是你不知道/学习是长远的, 不是~的事

重点词语和句式

1   有……之嫌 (to be accused of; to open oneself to the charge of; to give rise to the suspicion of; 嫌: 嫌疑)

    (1) 争论的焦点集中在……象征全球化的星巴克咖啡是否有侵犯中国五千年文化之嫌。
        (The debate focused on . . . whether Starbucks, a symbol of globalization, could be accused of invading five thousand years of Chinese culture.)

    (2) 这个电视节目宣传健康食品, 有做广告之嫌。
        (This television program promotes health food; it opens itself up to the charge of advertising such food.)

    (3) 他强调女人要留在家里做主妇、做母亲, 有人说他有歧视女性之嫌。
        (He emphasized that women should stay home to be housewives and mothers. Some people said that his words gave rise to the suspicion of sexual discrimination.)

用“有……之嫌”完成句子:

    (1) _____有自不量力之嫌。

    (2) _____有侵犯人民偷盗之嫌。

2   N年(月/星期/天) 之久 (as long as N years, months, weeks or days)

    (1) 2007 年 7 月, 在舆论的压力和网民的抗议之下, 已开设了七年之久的故宫星巴克咖啡正式撤出。
        (In July 2007, under pressure from public opinion and the protests of cybercitizens, the Starbucks which had been open in the Forbidden City for as long as seven years officially closed its doors.)

    (2) 那位歌星为演唱会准备了两个月之久。
        (That singer prepared for his concert for as long as two months.)

    (3) 暴风雪持续了三天之久。
        (The storm continued for as long as three days.)

翻译:

    (1) The tradition of celebrating the Chinese New Year is as old as three thousand years.

    _____

    (2) In March 2015, the TA strike at the University of Toronto lasted as long as three weeks.

    _____

3　别扭 (*bièniǔ* awkward; awkwardly)

    (1)　星巴克开在故宫, 好比宫女在宫装外面穿上比基尼一样让人别扭。
    (Opening a Starbucks in the Forbidden City was like putting a bikini over the palace robe of a lady-in-waiting. It was awkward.)

    (2)　这个句子读起来很别扭。
    (This sentence reads awkwardly.)

    (3)　穿西服、打领带让他很别扭。
    (He felt awkward wearing a suit and tie.)

翻译:

    (1)　I don't like this teapot. It has an awkward shape.

    _____

    (2)　On their first date, they both felt awkward.

    _____

4　面目全非 (to have changed beyond all recognition)

    (1)　北京现在已经面目全非, 有保存价值的古建筑几乎都拆光了, 取而代之的净是些灵气全无、喧宾夺主的大型现代建筑。
    (Now Beijing has changed beyond all recognition. Almost all of the ancient architecture which should have been preserved has been torn down. Instead, soulless and imposing modern buildings dominate the cityscape.)

    (2)　这座有100多年历史的建筑被大火烧得面目全非。
    (This 100-year-old building was destroyed beyond all recognition in a fire.)

    (3)　好久没回去, 昔日干净漂亮的校园已经面目全非。
    (I haven't been back for a long time. The clean, pretty campus of yesteryear has changed beyond all recognition.)

用"面目全非"完成对话:

    (1)　A: 老师喜欢你的文章吗?

        B: _____

    (2)　A: 车祸以后, 你的汽车还好吧?

        B: _____

5　取而代之 (instead; to replace something or someone)

    (1)　北京现在已经面目全非, 有保存价值的古建筑几乎都拆光了, 取而代之的净是些灵气全无、喧宾夺主的大型现代建筑。
    (Now Beijing has changed beyond all recognition. Almost all of the ancient architecture which should have been preserved has been torn down. Instead, soulless and imposing modern buildings dominate the cityscape.)

(2) 低矮破旧的小房子不见了,取而代之的是整齐漂亮的三层楼房。
(The decrepit little houses are all gone. In their places are neat and pretty three-story buildings.)

(3) 去年流行的黄色被今年的红色取而代之。
(Yellow has been replaced by red as this year's in-fashion color.)

用"取而代之"完成对话:

(1) A: 现在大家都不写信了。

B: _____

(2) A: 前几年的晚会主持人都是中年人, 今年呢?

B: _____

6　勾起……回忆 (to revive memories of)

(1) 故宫里的星巴克恰恰勾起了中国人对近代屈辱历史的痛苦回忆。
(What the Starbucks in the Forbidden City in fact did was revive the Chinese people's painful memories of humiliation from recent history.)

(2) 那些旧照勾起了他美好的回忆, 好像他又回到了家乡。
(Those old pictures revived wonderful memories. He seemed to have returned to his hometown.)

(3) 这首歌勾起了老人对青年时代的回忆。
(That song revived the old man's memories of his youth.)

翻译:

(1) She couldn't finish watching the movie because of the sad memories it brought back.

_____

(2) These old pictures always revive beautiful memories of my childhood.

_____

7　一味 (blindly; obsessively)

(1) 一味模仿甚至原样照抄就会成为邯郸学步。
(If we blindly imitated or even outright copied [the West], we would lose what makes us unique.)

(2) 他炒股票, 一味想发财。
(He speculates on stocks; he is obsessed with getting rich.)

(3) 有人为了减肥一味吃素, 这样对身体健康不利。
(To lose weight, some people obsessively eat only vegetables. As a result, their health suffers.)

用"一味"完成对话:

(1) A: 他追随时尚吗?

B: _____

(2) A: 那女孩喜欢照镜子。

　　B: _____

8　以……自居 (to claim to be . . .)

(1) 星巴克撤出故宫让那些以传统文化保护者自居的人们兴奋了一阵子。
(After Starbucks left the Forbidden City, those who claimed to be protectors of traditional culture were excited for a while.)

(2) 他虽然是大学教授, 但不以"学者"自居。
(Although he is a professor, he does not claim to be a scholar.)

(3) 他有妻子却以单身者自居, 老在网上骗女孩儿。
(He is married but claims to be single. He often dupes young women online.)

用"以……自居"完成对话:

(1) A: 他研究经济多年, 应该算是专家。

　　B: _____

(2) A: 那位领导平易近人, 跟普通人一样。

　　B: _____

9　涉及……问题 (to touch upon an issue)

(1) 这里面还涉及到另一个更敏感的问题, 那就是故宫这样的文化象征应不应该商业化。
(Here [the debate] touched upon a more sensitive issue: whether a cultural symbol like the Forbidden City should have been commercialized.)

(2) 这位教授的演讲涉及政治和文化问题。
(The professor's lecture touched upon both political and cultural issues.)

(3) 那位电影明星要求记者不要涉及个人感情问题。
(That movie star asked the reporters not to touch upon the issue of her private life.)

用"涉及……问题"完成对话:

(1) A: 这部电影主要说什么?

　　B: _____

(2) A: 我们应该尽量不使用塑料袋, 对吗?

　　B: _____

10　平息 (píngxī to die down; to overcome)

(1) 故宫之争平息不久, 2012 年 9 月星巴克在杭州灵隐寺景区开店, 随之再次引发新争议。
(Not long after the controversy over the Forbidden City died down, Starbucks opened a store in a scenic area of the Temple of the Soul's Retreat in Hangzhou in September 2012. A new controversy broke out soon thereafter.)

(2) 午夜, 暴风雨终于平息了, 星星在天空闪烁。
(At midnight, the storm finally died down. The stars twinkled in the sky.)

(3) 发现儿子吸毒以后，父亲无法平息心中的愤怒。
(After the father discovered that his son took drugs, he could not overcome his anger.)

用"平息"完成对话：

(1) A: 海上的风浪很大，我们能去游泳吗？

B: ＿＿＿＿＿＿＿＿＿＿＿＿＿＿＿＿＿＿＿＿＿

(2) A: 那两个兄弟吵了半天，双方都很激动。

B: ＿＿＿＿＿＿＿＿＿＿＿＿＿＿＿＿＿＿＿＿＿

11　持……的态度 (to adopt an attitude of; to hold a view of)

(1) 有人对此表示理解，一部人则持反对的态度。
(Some people [approved of the administrators' actions]; . . . others, however, held the opposite view.)

(2) 她总是对生活持乐观的态度。
(She always holds a positive view of life.)

(3) 新闻记者在政治上应该持中立的态度。
(Journalists should remain politically neutral.)

用"持……的态度"完成对话：

(1) A: 股票时升时跌，你对股市前景持什么态度？

B: ＿＿＿＿＿＿＿＿＿＿＿＿＿＿＿＿＿＿＿＿＿

(2) A: 对虎妈的教育方式，你怎么看？

B: ＿＿＿＿＿＿＿＿＿＿＿＿＿＿＿＿＿＿＿＿＿

练习

一. 根据课文, 回答问题

(1) 赞成星巴克进驻故宫的人持什么看法？
(2) 支持星巴克撤出故宫的人怎么说？
(3) 星巴克在灵隐寺景区开店为什么造成争议？

二. 至少用三个新词语回答以下每个问题, 请在新词语下面划出一道线

(1) 听说法国人抗议麦当劳进驻卢浮宫，你对此持什么态度？
(2) 有人提议把故宫里的小摊位搬出去，你怎么看？
(3) 你对让拉面馆、茶馆进驻故宫怎么看？
(4) 有人说灵隐寺幽静、古朴，充满商业味道的星巴克让千年古寺不中不西、不伦不类，你同意吗？

三. 写作练习

从讨论题中选择一题，写一篇短文，题目自己决定，字数: 500–700字。

四. 讨论

(1) 你认为故宫里该不该有美国的星巴克? 在别的国家有没有类似的争论?
(2) 你认为故宫里该不该有中国本土的拉面、茶馆? 故宫该不该进行商业开发?
(3) 你认为星巴克在故宫内开店与在灵隐寺外开店意义一样吗?
(4) 你认为麦当劳、沃尔玛 (*Wò'ěrmǎ* Walmart)、好莱坞 (*Hǎoláiwū* Hollywood) 电影等进入中国是不是对中国经济和文化传统的侵蚀?
(5) 你认为在全球化的大背景下, 如何保护本民族的文化传统、文化遗产?

五. 辩论

题目: 星巴克进入中国市场是文化侵略吗?
正方: 星巴克进入中国市场是文化侵略
反方: 星巴克进入中国市场不是文化侵略
辩论的内容可以考虑以下方面:

(1) 星巴克能够带来经济利益、使文化多元化吗?
(2) 在中国开设星巴克给各国游客提供更好的服务、更多的选择吗?
(3) 让星巴克进入中国市场体现中国文化的包容性、自信力吗?
(4) 星巴克破坏文化景点的整体性、带来人流量过大、影响文物保存吗?

第五单元

新与旧

第9课　光棍节与网购

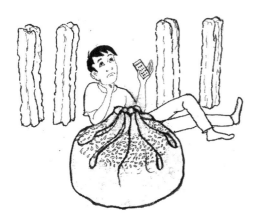

Figure 9.1 四根油条加一个包子
by Mingming Cheung (2020)

© Mingming Cheung.

Figure 9.2 全国上下都疯狂买、买、买
by Mingming Cheung (2020)

© Mingming Cheung.

Figure 9.3 2020年面临"老婆荒"
by Mingming Cheung (2020)

© Mingming Cheung.

Figure 9.4 出生性别比不平衡
by Mingming Cheung (2020)

© Mingming Cheung.

在中国，每年的11月11日被当今不少单身青年戏称为"光棍节"或者"单身节"。这个日子既和传统节日搭不上边，也和洋节没有半点关系。这是属于年轻人的娱乐性节日，他们以自己是单身为傲。光棍节这天的吉祥物是四根油条加一个包子，四根油条就是"11·11"中的四个"1"，包子是中间的那个点。

许多人认为，这个非法定的节日源于上世纪90年代，是当时南京大学的学生首次提出的。据说他们选中这一天，是因为用阿拉伯数字书写这个日期，4个"1"字形状酷似4个单身青年。

今天，在中国的城市，尤其像北京这样的大都会，单身不再是一种禁忌。在媒体和商家们的热炒下，"单身节"消费已成气候。花店老板、酒吧老板、以及其他行业的商人，都因为单身青年在11月11日肯花钱而大发其财。

在光棍节这天，什么也比不上网上购物那么疯狂。凌晨一到，不仅单身的人上网狂购，全国上下都"买买买"。这样的购物狂欢越演越烈：2014年"光棍节"，淘宝的天猫营业38分钟就达到了100亿的营业额，全天的营业额更达到了517亿人民币。

然而，在"光棍节"红火、热闹的背后，却隐藏着一个残酷的现实：到2020年，中国会面临"老婆荒"，数千万男青年会找不到老婆打光棍。

国家人口及家庭计划委员会称，中国出生婴儿性别比直逼120（平均每出生100名女婴就有近120名男婴出生），个别省份竟超过了130，大大偏离了103–107的正常值。居高不下的出生人口性别比有着复杂的社会背景。养儿防老的思想造成了人们的"男性偏好"，重男轻女的价值观使得两性社会地位不平等、女性在受教育和择业上受到歧视。

出生性别比的不平衡给社会带来严重隐患。首先会对男性过剩的婚姻市场造成压力，其次影响婚姻、家庭关系的和谐，并有可能危及人口安全、不利于社会稳定。设想如果数千万大龄青年找不到配偶，婚外恋、婚外性关系、非婚生育就不可避免；卖淫嫖娼、性犯罪、拐卖人口等现象就必然会增加，这些问题将对社会安定形成严峻挑战。

在商家和媒体热热闹闹地庆祝"光棍节"的同时，我们面对的是男女性别不平等的现状。我们希望政府从根本入手，解决这个问题。第一，强化舆论宣传，树立生男生女都一样的生育观；第二，建立健全的社会保障制度，尤其是解决农村居民的养老问题；第三，大力提高妇女的经济、社会地位，保护妇女儿童合法权利。只有这样才能有效地遏制人口男女比上升的趋势。

今天, 商家和媒体热火朝天地庆祝"光棍节"。将来, 即使不发生"老婆荒", 恐怕人们还会有各种各样的理由来庆祝单身节吧。

第9課 光棍節與網購

在中國, 每年的11月11日被當今不少單身青年戲稱為"光棍節"或者"單身節"。這個日子既和傳統節日搭不上邊,也和洋節沒有半點關係。這是屬於年輕人的娛樂性節日,他們以自己是單身為傲。光棍節這天的吉祥物是四根油條加一個包子,四根油條就是"11·11"中的四個"1",包子是中間的那個點。

許多人認為, 這個非法定的節日源於上世紀90年代,是當時南京大學的學生首次提出的。據說他們選中這一天,是因為用阿拉伯數字書寫這個日期,4個"1"字形狀酷似4個單身青年。

今天, 在中國的城市,尤其像北京這樣的大都會,單身不再是一種禁忌。在媒體和商家們的熱炒下,"單身節"消費已成氣候。花店老板、酒吧老板、以及其他行業的商人,都因為單身青年在11月11日肯花錢而大發其財。

在光棍節這天, 什麼也比不上網上購物那麼瘋狂。凌晨一到,不僅單身的人上網狂購,全國上下都"買買買"。這樣的購物狂歡越演越烈:2014年光棍節,淘寶的天貓38分鐘就達到了100億的營業額,全天的營業額更達到了517億人民幣。

然而, 在"光棍節"紅火、熱鬧的背後,卻隱藏著一個殘酷的現實:到2020年,中國會面臨"老婆荒",數千萬男青年會找不到老婆打光棍。

國家人口及家庭計劃委員會稱, 中國出生嬰兒性別比直逼120(平均每出生100名女嬰就有近120名男嬰出生),個別省份竟超過了130, 大大偏離了103–107的正常值。居高不下的出生人口性別比有著複雜的社會背景。養兒防老的思想造成了人們的"男性偏好",重男輕女的價值觀使得兩性社會地位不平等、女性在受教育和擇業上受到歧視。

出生性別比的不平衡給社會帶來嚴重隱患。首先會對男性過剩的婚姻市場造成壓力,其次影響婚姻、家庭關係的和諧,並有可能危及人口安全、不利于社會穩定。設想如果數千萬大齡青年找不到配偶,婚外戀、婚外性關係、非婚生育就不可避免;賣淫嫖娼、性犯罪、拐賣人口等現象就必然會增加,這些問題將對社會安定形成嚴峻挑戰。

在商家和媒體熱熱鬧鬧地慶祝"光棍節"的同時, 我們面對的是男女性別不平等的現狀。我們希望政府從根本入手,解決這個問題。第一, 強化輿論宣傳,樹立生男生女都一樣的生育觀;第二，建立健全的社會保障制度，尤其是解決農村居民的養老問題；第三，大力提高婦女的經濟、社會地位，保護婦女兒童合法權利。只有這樣才能有效地遏制人口男女比上升的趨勢。

今天，商家和媒體熱火朝天地慶祝"光棍節"。將來，即使不發生"老婆荒"，恐怕人們還會有各種各樣的理由來慶祝單身節吧。

新词语

网购	網購	wǎnggòu	online shopping ~商品/~价格
光棍	光棍	guānggùn	bachelor ~汉; 打~ (to remain a bachelor)
戏称	戲稱	xìchēng	to call jokingly; 开玩笑称作 有些人~纪录片《舌尖上的中国》为《减肥者的灾难》/认识他的人~他是"老狐狸"
娱乐性	娛樂性	yúlèxìng	recreational; amusement ~电影/~公园
吉祥物	吉祥物	jíxiángwù	symbol of good luck 北京奥运会的~是福娃/中国传统~包括龙 (lóng dragon)、凤 (fèng phoenix)、龟 (guī turtle)、麟 (lín unicorn)
油条	油條	yóutiáo	long, deep-fried, twisted sticks of dough 一根~
书写	書寫	shūxiě	to write; 写 (书面语) 用毛笔~/~练习
酷似	酷似	kùsì	to be exactly like 他长得~他哥哥
大都会	大都會	dàdūhuì	metropolis; 一百万人以上的大城市; metropolitan 温哥华、纽约都是有名的~/纽约~博物馆
禁忌	禁忌	jìnjì	taboo 春节的~/饮食的~/百无~
热炒	熱炒	rèchǎo	to market or promote (a product) using exaggerated claims or intense publicity; to hype; literally, to stir-fry; 媒体渲染、炒作 网络~/开发商~城中心的房地产
天猫	天貓	Tiānmāo	literally, "sky cat"; www.tmall.com is a website for commercial retail. A spinoff of Tabao淘宝, Tmall sells brand-name goods to consumers in China.
红火	紅火	hónghuǒ	booming; 很兴旺, 像火一般红 生意很~/他们的产品卖得很~
隐藏	隱藏	yǐncáng	to hide ~起来/~在背后
残酷	殘酷	cánkù	cruel 敌人很~/~的竞争
荒	荒	huāng	shortage; scarcity 油~/粮~
直逼	直逼	zhíbī	to approach; 逼近 人数~一百万/大葱价格~猪肉
个别	個別	gèbié	very few; 少数 ~人迟到/~地方供水不足
偏离	偏離	piānlí	to deviate; 离开正确的道路 ~方向/~中心
居高不下	居高不下	jū gāo bú xià	to remain high without any sign of falling; 没有下降的趋势 失业率~/房价一直~
偏好	偏好	piānhào	preference; to have a preference for something; 偏爱 他显示对艺术的~/消费者~便宜的商品
隐患	隱患	yǐnhuàn	hidden danger; 暗藏的祸患 存在安全~/带来~

设想	設想	shèxiǎng	to assume; to imagine; 假设; 想象 ~你是老师, 你会怎么做/失败的后果不堪~
配偶	配偶	pèi'ǒu	spouse 很多女性比~长寿/同性~
卖淫	賣淫	màiyín	prostitution; to prostitute oneself 禁止~/~罪/她因~被捕/她年轻时曾经~赚钱
嫖娼	嫖娼	piáochāng	to visit prostitutes 他赌博~, 无所不做
拐卖	拐賣	guǎimài	to kidnap and sell ~人口/~妇女
严峻	嚴峻	yánjùn	serious; severe; 严厉 ~的问题/~的考验
入手	入手	rùshǒu	to start with; 开始 从教育孩子~/不知从何~
树立	樹立	shùlì	to establish ~人生观/~好榜样
社会保障	社會保障	shèhuì bǎozhàng	social security 有关~的法律/~卡
遏制	遏制	èzhì	to keep within limits ~通货膨胀 (tōng huò péng zhàng inflation)/~腐败 (fǔbài corruption)
趋势	趨勢	qūshì	trend 教育发展的~/股票上升的~
热火朝天	熱火朝天	rè huǒ cháo tiān	enthusiastically; literally, hot flames [shooting] toward the sky 球迷~地为他们的球队加油/晚会上, 大家玩得~

重点词语和句式

1 A 和 B 搭不上边 (A does not have the slightest relationship to B; A does not have anything to do with B; someone is not . . . and is far from . . .)

(1) 这个日子既和传统节日搭不上边, 也和洋节没有半点关系。
(This day not only has nothing to do with traditional festivals, but also does not have the slightest relationship to Western festivals.)

(2) 这部电影和原著搭不上边。
(This movie does not have anything to do with the original book.)

(3) 她知道自己长得不出众, 跟美丽动人根本搭不上边。
(She knows that she does not stand out in a crowd and is far from beautiful.)

用"搭不上边"完成对话:

(1) A: 年轻人一般身体都很健康, 怎么会得这种癌、那种癌呢?

   B: _____

(2) A: 很多爱美的女孩子认为喝维C饮料能美容, 真的是这样吗?

   B: _____

2 以……为傲 (to be proud to; to take pride in)

(1) 这是属于年轻人的娱乐性节日, 他们以自己是单身为傲。
(This is a recreational festival for young people. They are proud to be single.)

(2) 她主张男女平等, 以身为女权主义者为傲。
(She advocates equality between men and women. She is proud to call herself a feminist.)

      (3) 那些志愿者以为社区工作为傲。

          (Those volunteers take pride in their community work.)

用"以……为傲"完成句子:

      (1) 他是他们村子第一个走出大山的大学生, _____

      (2) 父亲只是一个普通的工人, 可是 _____

3   源于 (to originate; to spring from; to come from)

      (1) 许多人认为, 这个非法定的节日源于上世纪90年代, 是当时南京大学的学生首次提出的。

          (Many people believe that this non-statutory holiday originated in the 1990s. The idea for the holiday might initially have come from students at Nanjing University.)

      (2) 有人说, 艺术源于生活。

          (Some people say that art springs from life.)

      (3) "Kindergarten" 这个英语单词源于德语。

          (The English word "kindergarten" comes from German.)

用"源于"完成句子:

      (1) 这位科学家的成功源于 _____

      (2) 这段婚姻的失败源于 _____

4   选中 (to choose something or someone)

      (1) 据说他们选中这一天, 是因为用阿拉伯数字书写这个日期, 4 个 "1" 字形状酷似 4 个单身青年。

          (It is said that they chose this day because when they used Arabic numerals to write the date, the four "1s" looked exactly like four bachelors.)

      (2) 他认识很多女孩儿, 选中的妻子竟然是她, 太出乎意料了。

          (He knows many girls. He unexpectedly chose her to be his wife; this came as a complete surprise.)

      (3) 在商店里, 她看了半天, 最后选中了那件粉红色的毛衣。

          (In the store, she looked around for a while and, in the end, chose that pink sweater.)

翻译:

      (1) We chose him because he was the best candidate for the job.

      _____

      (2) He knows how to invest in the stock market. The stocks that he picks always go up in value.

      _____

5　成气候 (to become an unavoidable part; to become an unalterable fact of life; to become a reality)

(1) 在媒体的热炒下,"单身节"消费已成气候。
(Thanks to media hype, consumption has become an unavoidable part of the "Singles' Festival.")

(2) 留学人员归国日益增多, 国内大公司想方设法吸引"海归"已成气候。
(More and more students who study abroad are returning home to work. That employers must make efforts to attract these "returnees" has become an unalterable fact of life.)

(3) 房地产市场已进入稳定发展, 楼价疯涨难成气候。
(The real estate market had entered a period of stable growth. The soaring property values that some people had hoped for would not become a reality.)

用"成气候"完成句子:

(1) A: 现在智能手机很普及, 大家都用手机阅读吗?

　　B: _____

(2) A: 有些专家分析, 大学生创业不容易, 你说呢?

　　B: _____

6　危及 (to threaten; to endanger)

(1) 出生性别比的不平衡……有可能危及人口安全, 不利于社会稳定。
(The imbalance in the birth sex ratio . . . could threaten the security of the population and undermine social stability.)

(2) 2016 年加拿大艾伯塔省森林火灾面积扩大, 危及萨斯喀彻温省。
(In 2016, forest fires in the Canadian province of Alberta spread to threaten neighboring Saskatchewan.)

(3) 连续三年的干旱已经危及到这个地区几十万人的生存。
(For three consecutive years, the drought has endangered the lives of hundreds of thousands of people in the region.)

翻译:

(1) 巴西总统说, 兹卡病毒的爆发不会危及2016年8月举行的奥运会。

_____

(2) 有些医生警告, 滥用大麻 (marijuana) 影响健康, 甚至会危及生命。

_____

7　不利于 (to undermine; to harm; not conducive to)

(1) 出生性别比的不平衡……有可能危及人口安全, 不利于社会稳定。
(The imbalance in the birth sex ratio . . . could threaten the security of the population and undermine social stability.)

(2) 工作压力过大不利于身心健康。
(Too much work stress can harm a person's physical and mental health.)

(3) 房价过快上涨不利于房地产市场的稳定发展。
(The rapid rise in housing prices is not conducive to the stable development of the real estate market.)

用"不利于"完成对话:

(1) A: 他们快五十岁才有了这个孩子, 能不溺爱吗?

B: _____

(2) A: 小丽比以前瘦了很多, 听说她一天只吃一根香蕉。

B: _____

练习

一. 根据课文, 回答问题

(1) 请介绍一下中国的"光棍节"。
(2) "光棍节"这个节日背后隐藏着什么样的社会现实?
(3) 中国出生人口性别比失衡, 原因有哪些?
(4) 出生人口性别比居高不下会对社会有什么样的影响?

二.用以下每题所给的词语或句式完成对话

(1) A: 你听说过光棍节吗?

B: _____
(娱乐性 以……为傲 禁忌)

(2) A: 有的人老是上网购物。

B: _____
(热炒 红火 残酷)

(3) A: 你太重男轻女了。

B: _____
(偏好 寄托 设想)

(4) A: 出生性别比不平衡的问题如何解决?

B: _____
(不利于 社会保障 健全)

三.写作练习

你是一个人口问题专家, 写一篇关于性别比失衡的文章, 呼吁社会和政府高度重视这个问题。字数: 500–700 字。

四.讨论

(1) 你对中国的"光棍节"怎么看？如果你是中国的一个单身青年，你会不会庆祝"光棍节"？

(2) 中国的"光棍节"已经成为购物狂欢节，在别的国家有没有什么节日也是这样？

(3) 在各个国家，大龄男女怎么找对象最合适？

(4) 请在网上查一查，在别的国家有没有"老婆荒"或是"男人荒"的问题。

(5) 请在中文网站找一篇文章，介绍一下中国政府或者一个地方政府怎样遏制性别比升高的趋势。

五. 辩论

题目: 做男人难还是做女人难？

正方: 做男人比做女人难

反方: 做女人比做男人难

辩论内容可以考虑以下方面:

(1) 重男轻女的观念影响男孩与女孩在家庭中的地位吗？

(2) 男女在智慧和体力上一样吗？

(3) 要是男女有同等学历、同等工作能力，他们有同等机会发展事业吗？

(4) 结婚以后，男女同样工作、同样养家、同样分担家务劳动、照顾子女吗？

(5) 在面对压力、挫折时，就外表和内心而言，男人坚强还是女人坚强？

第10课　微信与中国新经济

Figure 10.1 从六岁儿童到八旬老翁，拿起微信都可以轻松上手
by Mingming Cheung (2020)
© Mingming Cheung.

Figure 10.2 据《纽约时报》报道
by Mingming Cheung (2020)
© Mingming Cheung.

Figure 10.3 路边卖煎饼的小贩，也可以用微信支付
by Mingming Cheung (2020)
© Mingming Cheung.

Figure 10.4 以人为本
by Mingming Cheung (2020)
© Mingming Cheung.

　　近四十年来，中国经历了一波又一波巨大变化。从 1978 年开始，中国用了二十年时间成为世界工厂；自 1990 年以来，中国大搞基础建设；最近十年来，随着科技创新和产品质量的提升，中国涌现出更多新的经济现象，其中最引人注目的就是微信的流行。微信是由腾讯公司研发的移动通讯软件。2011 年 1 月 21 日该软件推出以后，微信用户就一直迅猛增长：2012 年 3 月底为 1 亿，2017 年 5 月达到了 9.38 亿。这个数字还在不断增长之中，也许在不久的将来，14 亿中国人都会成为微信用户。中国会成为一个全民进入互联网的社会。据《纽约时报》报道，微信已经成为领先的通讯软件。连流行全世界的脸书，在很多方面都落后于微信。

　　说今天的中国是微信的时代，一点也不夸张。在中国，几乎每部手机上都安装着微信，家家都有微信群。大到学校、公司和政府，都用微信办公；小到路边卖煎饼的小摊，也可以用微信支付。就像腾讯的宣传口号所说，"微信是一种生活方式"：微信确确实实已经成为当代中国的运行平台，是当代中国社会、经济、生活必不可少的网络工具。

　　微信的流行离不开其强大的功能。微信是通讯工具：它可以收发文字、语音、图片和视频，也可以语音、视频通话；微信是社交助手：你可以扫码加新朋友、轻松实现多人群聊，还可以在朋友圈上展示个人生活；微信是工作利器：你可以通过聊天群开会，还可以轻松收发文件；微信是新闻平台：从本地的小道消息到国家大事，微信上都有；微信是购物平台：你可以使用微信支付、结账，可以通过它网购、订餐、买公交地铁票、预订机票和旅馆；微信还是娱乐场所：闲时你可以看看朋友圈，玩玩游戏。

　　如果说上面提到的功能并不是微信的创新，那么微信的成功在于它拥有一种中国文化特有的亲和性。微信把手机用户最需要的功能都整合到一起，并且做到了简单易用。从六岁儿童到八旬老翁，拿起微信都可以轻松上手，很快就能熟练使用。微信处处为人着想，主动适应用户而不是强迫用户去适应它。这种亲和性消除了科技产品和人之间的距离。在微信上交流，快速、即时、即兴，没有技术障碍。

　　微信突出了中国新经济的特征，那就是技术的提升和亲和性相结合。过去四十年中国经济的高速发展有目共睹，尤其是近十年来，由科技行业领军的新经济发展更是日新月异，天翻地覆。最新科技在产品开发以及服务设计中全面运用，没有让新经济与普通民众的日常生活疏远，相反，新经济由于其亲和性，深深地融入了大众生活。中国新经济的亲和性源于中国传统文化特有的"以人为本"的思想。中国企业家追求创新，同时要求产品的实用性；他们讲究速度，也注重为客户提供便利；他们追求利润，也致力于降低价格，让大家消费得起；他们注重产品质量，也关心用户体验。他们在现代商业中创造出传统中国文化特有的体贴和亲民。

中国的科技产业体现着这种新经济的特征。以华为、小米、一加为代表的中国智能手机制造商，制造出物美价廉的手机：质量上能媲美苹果、三星，价格上又十分亲民，让中国人手一部手机成为可能。中国几大电信商把网络铺设到每个村，并把电信价格降低到低收入人口都用得起的程度。中国的高铁里程比全世界的高铁里程加起来还要长，马上就要实现县县通高速公路、市市通高铁和飞机的目标。中国电子商务中最有影响力的网站阿里巴巴，商品包罗万象，质优价廉。以上这些科技产业相叠加的结果是，不管你身处何地，从一份订单从手机上发出，到你从快递小哥手里接过邮包，最多只需要五天。如果说十年、二十年前中国还是一个落后的国家，那么今天从西方去中国的人往往会感慨，中国在基础设施和电子商务方面，已经把很多西方发达国家远远抛在身后。

微信时代的中国，不仅生产廉价消费品，还制造高端科技产品，并且将传统文化中的亲和性注入经济发展中。如果说作为世界工厂的中国提高了全世界的生活质量，那么微信时代的中国新经济，也许会影响我们这个世界的生活方式。

第10課 微信與中國新經濟

近四十年來，中國經歷了一波又一波巨大變化。從1978年開始，中國用了二十年時間成為世界工廠；自1990年以來，中國大搞基礎建設；最近十年來，隨著科技創新和產品質量的提升，中國湧現出更多新的經濟現象，其中最引人註目的就是微信的流行。微信是由騰訊公司研發的移動通訊軟件。2011年1月21日該軟件推出以後，微信用戶就一直迅猛增長：2012年3月底為1億，2017年5月達到了9.38億。這個數字還在不斷增長之中，也許在不久的將來，14億中國人都會成為微信用戶。中國會成為一個全民進入互聯網的社會。據《紐約時報》報道，微信已經成為領先的通訊軟件。連流行全世界的臉書，在很多方面都落後於微信。

說今天的中國是微信的時代，一點也不誇張。在中國，幾乎每部手機上都安裝著微信，家家都有微信群。大到學校、公司和政府，都用微信辦公；小到路邊賣煎餅的小攤，也可以用微信支付。就像騰訊的宣傳口號所說，"微信是一種生活方式"：微信確確實實已經成為當代中國的運行平臺，是當代中國社會、經濟、生活必不可少的網絡工具。

微信的流行離不開其強大的功能。微信是通訊工具：它可以收發文字、語音、圖片和視頻，也可以語音、視頻通話；微信是社交助手：你可以掃碼加新朋友、輕鬆實現多人群聊，還可以在朋友圈上展示個人生活；微信是工作利器：你可以通過聊天群開會，還可以輕鬆收發文件；微信是新聞平臺：從本地的小道消息到國家大事，微信上都有；微信是購物平臺：你可以使用微信支付、結賬，可以通過它網購、訂餐、買公交地鐵票、預訂機票和旅館；微信還是娛樂場所：閑時你可以看看朋友圈，玩玩遊戲。

如果說上面提到的功能並不是微信的創新，那麼微信的成功在於它擁有一種中國文化特有的親和性。微信把手機用戶最需要的功能都整合到一起，並且做到了簡單易用。從六歲兒童到八旬老翁，拿起微信都可以輕鬆上手，很快就能熟練使用。微信處處為人着想，主動適應用戶而不是強迫用戶去適應它。這種親和性消除了科技產品和人之間的距離。在微信上交流，快速、即時、即興，沒有技術障礙。

微信體現了中國新經濟的特徵，那就是技術的提升和親和性相結合。過去四十年中國經濟的高速發展有目共睹，尤其是近十年來，由科技行業領軍的新經濟發展更是日新月異，天翻地覆。最新科技在產品開發以及服務設計中全面運用，沒有讓新經濟與普通民眾的日常生活疏遠，相反，新經濟由於其親和性，深深地融入了大眾生活。中國新經濟的親和性源於中國傳統文化特有的“以人為本”的思想。中國企業家追求創新，同時要求產品的實用性；他們講究速度，也注重為客戶提供便利；他們追求利潤，也致力於降低價格，讓大家消費得起；他們注重產品質量，也關心用戶體驗。他們在現代商業中創造出傳統中國文化特有的體貼和親民。

中國的科技產業體現著這種新經濟的特徵。以華為、小米、一加為代表的中國智能手機制造商，制造出物美價廉的手機：質量上能媲美蘋果、三星，價格上又十分親民，讓中國人手一部手機成為可能。中國幾大電信商把網絡鋪設到每個村，並把電信價格降低到低收入人口都用得起的程度。中國的高鐵里程比全世界的高鐵里程加起來還要長，馬上就要實現縣縣通高速公路、市市通高鐵和飛機的目標。中國電子商務中最有影響力的網站阿里巴巴，商品包羅萬象，質優價廉。以上這些科技產業相疊加的結果是，不管你身處何地，一份訂單從手機上發出，到你從快遞小哥手裏接過郵包，最多只需要五天。如果說十年、二十年前中國還是一個落後的國家, 那麼今天從西方去中國的人往往會感慨, 中國在基礎設施和電子商務方面, 已經把很多西方發達國家遠遠拋在身後。

　　微信時代的中國, 不僅生產廉價消費品, 還制造高端科技產品, 並且將傳統文化中的親和性注入經濟發展中。如果說作為世界工廠的中國提高了全世界的生活質量, 那麼微信時代的中國新經濟, 也許會影響我們這個世界的生活方式。

新词语

微信	微信	Wēixìn	WeChat, literally, "micro-message," was developed by Tencent. It is China's multipurpose messaging and mobile payment app.
科技	科技	kējì	science and technology 高~/~中心
创新	創新	chuàngxīn	innovation 勇于~/毫无~
腾讯	騰訊	Téngxùn	Tencent, literally, "soaring news," is a Chinese investment conglomerate whose subsidiaries specialize in various internet-related services and products.
通讯	通訊	tōngxùn	communication 我们都有手机, ~很方便/地震以后~中断
软件	軟件	ruǎnjiàn	software ~下载/~功能
该	該	gāi	that; 那个; it refers to the thing or person mentioned before 如果你在加拿大, 你得去中国驻~国大使馆申请旅游签证
互联网	互聯網	hùliánwǎng	the internet 公布在~上/~用户
领先	領先	lǐngxiān	to be in the lead 在比赛中~/在技术上~
脸书	臉書	Liǎnshū	Facebook ~是美国的一个社交服务网站
夸张	誇張	kuāzhāng	to exaggerate 过分~/有点~
安装	安裝	ānzhuāng	to install ~空调/~防盗报警器
群	羣	qún	group 脸书~组/~聊
煎饼	煎餅	jiānbǐng	a breakfast pancake rolled with a piece of deep-fried dough inside ~馃子
支付	支付	zhīfù	to pay 扫码~/微信~
宣传	宣傳	xuānchuán	publicity; to publicize 环保~/~风力发电
口号	口號	kǒuhào	slogan 喊~/反战~/爱国~
运行平台	運行平台	yùnxíng píngtái	operating platform 新系统的~/建立~
视频	視頻	shìpín	video ~游戏/~聊天
扫码	掃碼	sǎomǎ	to scan the code ~购买/~下载
利器	利器	lìqì	efficient instrument; weapon 文字是宣传的~/旅客不能携带~
结账	結賬	jiézhàng	to pay one's bill 到收款台~/饭后准备~

亲和性	親和性	qīnhéxìng	friendliness and tolerance 友爱包容的性质 有~的人善解人意、乐于助人
整合	整合	zhěnghé	to integrate ~学习的内容/把两个项目~成一个
旬	旬	xún	a period of ten years in a person's life 年过五~/七~老人
老翁	老翁	lǎowēng	old man; 翁: 老头儿 让座给一位~
适应	適應	shìyìng	to adapt ~新环境/~大学生活
消除	消除	xiāochú	to eliminate ~烦恼/~贫穷
即时	即時	jíshí	immediate; immediately 进行~交流/~解决问题
即兴	即興	jíxìng	impromptu; 因当前的感受而引起 ~表演/~演讲
体现	體現	tǐxiàn	to reflect 那幅画~了画家对大自然的热爱/这本书~了作者的智慧
障碍	障礙	zhàng'ài	obstacle 学习~/克服~
领军	領軍	lǐngjūn	to lead; leading ~前进/~人物
日新月异	日新月異	rì xīn yuè yì	to change with each passing day; 每天都有新发展, 每月都有变化 现代科技~/适应~的环境
天翻地覆	天翻地覆	tiān fān dì fù	a state of extreme confusion or total disorder; literally, the sky and the earth turn upside down ~的大事/闹得~
开发	開發	kāifā	development; to develop 自然资源~/软件~/~无人机的应用/~网络课程
其	其	qí	third-person pronoun; its; it; his; he; their; they ~味无穷/任~自然/夸大~词/各得~所/两人同心, ~利断金/~奈我何
融入	融入	róngrù	to integrate; integration ~新环境/~大自然/新移民的~/科技的~
以人为本	以人為本	yǐ rén wéi běn	people-oriented; literally, to regard people as essential ~的图书馆服务/~的社区发展
追求	追求	zhuīqiú	to pursue; pursuit ~完美/~名利/对爱情的~/拒绝追求者的~
实用性	實用性	shíyòngxìng	usefulness 有些建筑美观但是~不足/当今教育偏向~
速度	速度	sùdù	speed 加快~/放慢~
客户	客戶	kèhù	client 为~提供服务/赢得~的满意
利润	利潤	lìrùn	profit 花费小而~多/~上升/~下降
体贴	體貼	tǐtiē	thoughtfulness; to give every care to 表示~/对长辈的~/~父母/~家人
亲民	親民	qīnmín	putting people first; literally, to be close to the masses ~作风/~形象
华为	華為	Huáwéi	Huawei Technologies Co., Ltd. is a Chinese company which manufactures telecommunications equipment. It was founded in 1987.
小米	小米	Xiǎomǐ	Xiaomi, Inc. is China's largest smartphone manufacturer. It released its first smartphone in 2011.

一加	一加	Yìjiā	OnePlus is a Chinese smartphone manufacturer. It was founded in 2013.
智能手机	智能手機	zhìnéng shǒujī	smartphone 新款~/强功能~
电信商	電信商	diànxìnshāng	telecom carriers 中国电信、中国网通、中国联通都是中国~
铺设	鋪設	pūshè	to lay out ~两条铁路/~下水道
高铁	高鐵	gāotiě	high-speed rail 乘坐~/~列车
里程	里程	lǐchéng	mileage 这部车~少, 可以买/我经常坐这家航空公司的飞机, 积累 (jīlěi to accumulate)了很多~
电子商务	電子商務	diànzǐ shāngwù	e-commerce ~活动/~网站
阿里巴巴	阿里巴巴	Ālǐbābā	Alibaba Group is a Chinese e-commerce conglomerate. It was founded in 1999.
相叠加	相疊加	xiāng dié jiā	to superimpose 有时中秋国庆假期~/三种颜色~形成了另一种颜色
快递	快遞	kuàidì	express delivery 用~把包裹寄过去/收到~
基础	基礎	jīchǔ	basic; foundation ~研究/~知识/数学/英语~
设施	設施	shèshī	facility 安全~/医疗~
抛在身后	抛在身後	pāo zài shēn hòu	to leave behind 把烦恼~/把过去~
廉价	廉價	liánjià	low-cost ~飞机票/~小旅店
高端科技	高端科技	gāoduān kējì	high-end technology ~人才/发展~

重点词语和句式

1 一波又一波 (wave after wave)

(1) 近四十年来, 中国经历了一波又一波巨大变化。
(In the past forty years, China has experienced wave after wave of colossal changes.)

(2) 他遇到一波又一波的挫折, 但是他依然勇敢地追求成为艺术家的理想。
(He has encountered wave after wave of setbacks, but he still bravely pursues his dream of becoming an artist.)

(3) 这几天多伦多大学各个学院举行毕业典礼, 一波又一波的学生穿着黑袍参加典礼。
(In the past few days, the colleges of the University of Toronto have been holding graduation ceremonies. Wave after wave of students in black robes have been participating in the ceremonies.)

用"一波又一波"完成对话:

(1) A: 那部有关外星人的科幻片受欢迎吗?

B: _____

(2) A: 上个星期你去了一场演奏会。钢琴家结束演奏时, 观众热烈地鼓掌吗?

B: _____

2   相结合 (wedding; to combine)

(1) 微信体现了中国新经济的特征, 那就是技术的提升和亲和性相结合。
(WeChat reflects a characteristic of China's new economy, namely, the wedding of technological growth with consideration for human well-being.)

(2) 她把中国传统京剧和现代舞相结合, 开创出自己的表演风格。
(She combined traditional Peking opera with modern dance and created her own performing style.)

(3) 这件晚礼服是古典优雅和现代风格相结合, 真是漂亮。
(This evening gown combines classic elegance with modern style. It is really beautiful.)

用"相结合"完成对话:

(1) A: 你信中医还是西医？

B: _____

(2) A: 人要成功, 哪个重要？努力还是运气？

B: _____

3   有目共睹 (yǒu mù gòng dǔ to be obvious to all; 有眼睛的人都能看到, 比喻很明显)

(1) 过去四十年中国经济的高速发展[大家]有目共睹。
(The rapid development of China's economy over the past four decades is obvious to all.)

(2) 他在科学上的成就, 有目共睹, 令人钦佩。
(His achievements in science are obvious to all and truly admirable.)

(3) 她事业上的成功来之不易, 她的努力勤奋是有目共睹的。
(Her career success was hard-earned; her diligence was obvious to all.)

翻译:

(1) 他的见义勇为有目共睹, 值得表扬。

_____

(2) He is a capable manager. That his decisions have increased the company's profits is clear to all.

_____

4   致力于 (to commit oneself to; to devote oneself to; 集中精力在某方面)

(1) [中国企业者]追求利润, 也致力于降低价格, 让大家消费得起。
([Chinese business leaders] are driven by the desire to make profits, but are also committed to keeping prices low for the sake of consumer affordability.)

(2) 他是文学家, 致力于研究明清小说。
(He is a literature specialist. He has devoted his career to researching fiction of the Ming and Qing dynasties.)

(3) 丈夫死后, 她致力于子女的教育。
(After her husband's death, she devoted herself to educating her children.)

用"致力于"完成对话:

(1) A: 她此生事业成功吗？

　　B: _____

(2) A: 张医生是名医。他除了治疗还进行研究吗？

　　B: _____

5　媲美 (*pìměi* to be on a par with)

(1) 以华为、小米、一加为代表的中国智能手机制造商, 制造出物美价廉的手机: 质量上能媲美苹果、三星, 价格上又十分亲民, 让人手一部手机成为可能。
(China's smartphone manufacturers are represented by Huawei, Xiaomi and One-Plus. These companies have produced well-made, low-priced cellphones. In terms of quality, these cellphones are on a par with those manufactured by Apple and Samsung. Their prices are affordable and have made it possible for each and every Chinese to own a cellphone.)

(2) 你做的这道菜非常美味, 可以媲美山珍海味。
(The dish you made is delicious; it is on a par with the greatest delicacies in the world.)

(3) 他的豪宅非常华丽, 可以媲美皇宫。
(His mansion is magnificent; it is on a par with a palace.)

用"媲美"完成对话:

(1) A: 那个小姑娘唱歌真好听。

　　B: _____

(2) A: 哪家中国大学最有名？

　　B: _____

6　人手一 + measure word (each and every person with something in hand; 人人手中都拿着一种东西, 形容这种东西很受欢迎)

(1) 以华为、小米、一加为代表的中国智能手机制造商, 制造出物美价廉的手机: 质量上能媲美苹果、三星, 价格上又十分亲民, 让人手一部手机成为可能。
(China's smartphone manufacturers are represented by Huawei, Xiaomi and One-Plus. These companies have produced well-made, low-priced cellphones. In terms of quality, these cellphones are on a par with those manufactured by Apple and Samsung. Their prices are affordable and have made it possible for each and every Chinese to own a cellphone.)

(2) 只要去多伦多大学东亚图书馆, 你就会看到学生们人手一本书。
(If you went to the East Asian Library at the University of Toronto, you would see students, each and every one with a book in hand.)

(3) 那个冰淇淋店顾客满堂, 人手一杯冰淇淋。
(That ice cream shop is filled with customers, each and every one with a cup of ice cream in hand.)

用"人手一 + measure word"完成句子:

(1) A: 什么地方的人最爱喝珍珠奶茶?

　　B: ＿＿＿＿＿＿＿＿＿＿＿＿＿＿＿＿＿＿＿＿

(2) A: 这一大箱苹果够整个公司员工吃吗?

　　B: ＿＿＿＿＿＿＿＿＿＿＿＿＿＿＿＿＿＿＿＿

7　包罗万象 (bāo luó wàn xiàng a wide variety of; countless; 原意是包括一切景象, 形容内容丰富, 应有尽有)

(1) 中国电子商务最有影响力的网站阿里巴巴, 商品包罗万象, 质优价廉。
(The most influential Chinese e-commerce website is Alibaba. It sells a wide variety of high-quality, affordable merchandise.)

(2) 这本百科全书包罗万象, 从文学、历史到数学、物理什么都有。
(This encyclopedia covers a wide range of subjects; it has everything from literature and history to mathematics and physics.)

(3) 多伦多大学图书馆的书包罗万象, 什么种类都有。
(The University of Toronto Libraries have books on countless subjects.)

用"包罗万象"完成对话:

(1) A: 你们动物园里动物多不多?

　　B: ＿＿＿＿＿＿＿＿＿＿＿＿＿＿＿＿＿＿＿＿

(2) A: 你常在网络上搜索资料吗?

　　B: ＿＿＿＿＿＿＿＿＿＿＿＿＿＿＿＿＿＿＿＿

练习

一. 根据课文, 回答问题

(1) 你都是从哪些途径了解中国的? 西方媒体是怎么报道中国的?
(2) 你用过中国生产的产品吗? 你对中国的产品有什么印象?
(3) 你听说过中国的高铁吗? 比较你的国家的铁路系统与中国的高铁。
(4) 你用什么社交媒体? 介绍你使用社交媒体的经验和故事。

二. 至少用三个新词语回答以下每个问题, 请在新词语下面划出一道线

(1) 做调查后, 向全班介绍你的国家使用社交媒体的人口在过去二十年的增长状况。
(2) 你使用什么手机? 你用手机做什么? 手机在你生活中起到什么作用?
(3) 请比较网购和在商店购物不同的地方。
(4) 你去过中国吗? 讲讲你对中国印象最深的地方, 或者你在中国碰到的趣事。

三. 写作练习

题目:《科技与我》字数: 500–700 字。

下笔以前, 请考虑以下方面:

(1) 我们处在一个什么样的时代? 科技对这个时代有什么样的影响?
(2) 你成长的过程中, 电脑、互联网、社交媒体和手机等新科技对你有什么影响? 对你的影响和对你父辈或祖辈的影响有什么不同?
(3) 你对科技的态度是什么? 科技给你带来什么样的好处、什么样的坏处?

四. 讨论

(1) 经济有没有文化特征? 你国家的产品和服务与中国的产品和服务有什么不同?
(2) 你认为最理想的生活是什么样的? 和技术有没有关系?
(3) 新技术对学习有什么影响? 哪些是正面的? 哪些是负面的? 你希望我们的课程中怎么使用新技术? 你觉得学校应该采用哪些新技术?
(4) 调查后, 讨论世界经济的未来会是什么样的。

五. 辩论

题目: 未来会更好还是更糟?

正方: 未来会更好

反方: 未来会更糟

辩论内容可以考虑以下方面:

(1) 如果以历史为镜子的话, 现在的社会和过去的社会有什么不同, 社会总是越变越好吗?
(2) 什么样的生活对于人来说是好的, 什么是坏的?
(3) 科技对未来有什么正面和负面的影响?
(4) 哪些因素影响到人类和世界的未来?

Index of key expressions and sentence patterns
重点词语和句式索引

Vocabulary index
词语表

Ālǐbābā, 阿里巴巴, Alibaba Group is a Chinese e-commerce conglomerate. It was founded in 1999. L10, p.115

àixīn, 爱心, loving heart; compassion, L5, p.49

ānfǔ, 安抚, to calm, L6, p.60

ānquándài, 安全带, seat belt, L2, p.17, p.14

ān rán wú yàng, 安然无恙, safe and sound, L6, p.60

ānzhuāng, 安装, to install, L10, p.114

Àosīwéixīn, 奥斯维辛, Auschwitz, L8, p.88

Bāguó Liánjūn, 八国联军, Eight-Nation Alliance, L8, p.88

bǎishè, 摆设, objects on display; ornaments, L2, p.15

bànlǚ, 伴侣, partners, L3, p.26

bāoróng, 包容, tolerance; to tolerate, L8, p.88

bǎocún, 保存, to preserve, L8, p.88

bàojǐng, 报警, to report an emergency to the police, L5, p.51

bàozhà, 爆炸, to explode, L8, p.88

bèi, 倍, to double; times, L6, p.60

bèipàn, 背叛, to betray, L8, p.88

Bèi Yùmíng, 贝聿铭, Leoh Ming Pei (1917–2019), commonly known as I. M. Pei, is a Chinese-born American architect. L8, p.88

běnnéng fǎnyìng, 本能反应, instinctive reaction, L6, p.60

běntǔ, 本土, one's native country or land, L8, p.89

béng, 甭, don't, L7, p.72

bèng, 蹦, to hop; to jump; to bounce, L7, p.73

bǐjīní, 比基尼, bikini, L8, p.88

bìjìng, 毕竟, after all, L2, p.14

bǐngchí, 秉持, to uphold, L6, p.60

bōlí, 玻璃, glass, L8, p.88

bú luò sú tào, 不落俗套, not to conform to conventions, L6, p.60

bú qiè shíjì, 不切实际, unrealistic or impractical, L7, p.72

bùguǐ, 不轨, not in accordance with the law; literally, straying from the proper path, L2, p.14

bù jué yú ěr, 不绝于耳, (of sound) to remain vibrating in the ears, L8, p.88

bù kě wǎnhuí, 不可挽回, irreparable, L5, p.50

bù lún bú lèi, 不伦不类, neither fish nor fowl, L8, p.88

bùyī, 不一, different; not the same, L3, p.26

bù zhī suǒ cuò, 不知所措, to be at a loss as to what to do, L6, p.60

cǎifǎng, 采访, to have an interview with; interview, L3, p.26

cāoláo, 操劳, to work hard, L7, p.72

cánjí, 残疾, physical disability; physically handicapped, L5, p.50

cánkù, 残酷, cruel, L9, p.104

cǎnliè, 惨烈, severe, L6, p.60

chāduì, 插队, to cut the line, L2, p.14

chāi, 拆, to dismantle; to tear apart, L8, p.88

chángnián, 常年, all year round; year in and year out, L3, p.26

Chángqí, 长崎, Nagasaki, L8, p.88

chàngdǎo, 倡导, to advocate, L5, p.51

chàngyìshū, 倡议书, written proposal, L7, p.72

chè, 撤, to withdraw; to evacuate; to remove, L8, p.89

chèlí, 撤离, to evacuate, L6, p.60

chén āi luò dìng, 尘埃落定, to settle; to end; literally, the dust settles, L5, p.51

chéngběn, 成本, prime cost, L2, p.14

chéngdān, 承担, to bear; to undertake, L5, p.50

chéngqīng, 澄清, to clarify, L5, p.51

chōng, 冲, to dash, L6, p.60

chōngshí, 充实, to enrich; to expand one's horizons; fulfilling, L7, p.73

chōngtū, 冲突, conflict, L8, p.88

chóngbài, 崇拜, to worship; worship, L2, p.13

chóng yáng mèi wài, 崇洋媚外, to worship everything foreign and to be subservient to foreigners, L7, p.72

chū rén yì liào, 出人意料, unexpected; to come as a surprise, L4, p.36

chuánchéng, 传承, to pass on, L7, p.73

chuàngxīn, 创新, innovation, L10, p.114